Street by Street

C000126553

EXETER

BUDLEIGH SALTERTON, EXMOUTH, TOPSHAM,

Clyst St Mary, Cowley, Dawlish Warren, Exminster, Exton, Lympstone, Poltimore, Starcross, Woodbury

3rd edition February 2006
© Automobile Association Developments Limited 2006

Original edition printed May 2001

Ordnance Survey® This product includes map data licensed from Ordnance Survey® with the permission of the Controller of Her Majesty's Stationery Office. © Crown copyright 2006. All rights reserved. Licence number 399221.

All rights reserved. No part of this publication may be reproduced, stored in a retrieval system, or transmitted in any form or by any means – electronic, mechanical, photocopying, recording or otherwise – unless the permission of the publisher has been given beforehand.

Published by AA Publishing (a trading name of Automobile Association Developments Limited, whose registered office is Fanum House, Basing View, Basingstoke, Hampshire RG21 4EA. Registered number 1878835).

Mapping produced by the Cartography Department of The Automobile Association. (A02654)

A CIP Catalogue record for this book is available from the British Library.

Printed by Oriental Press in Dubai

The contents of this atlas are believed to be correct at the time of the latest revision. However, the publishers cannot be held responsible or liable for any loss or damage occasioned to any person acting or refraining from action as a result of any use or reliance on any material in this atlas, nor for any errors, omissions or changes in such material. This does not affect your statutory rights. The publishers would welcome information to correct any errors or omissions and to keep this atlas up to date. Please write to Publishing, The Automobile Association, Fanum House (FH12), Basing View, Basingstoke, Hampshire, RG21 4EA.

Ref: ML109y

Key to map pages ii-iii
Key to map symbols iv-1
Enlarged map pages 2-3
Main map pages 4-45
Index – towns & villages 46
Index – streets 46-50
Index – featured places 50-51
Acknowledgements 51

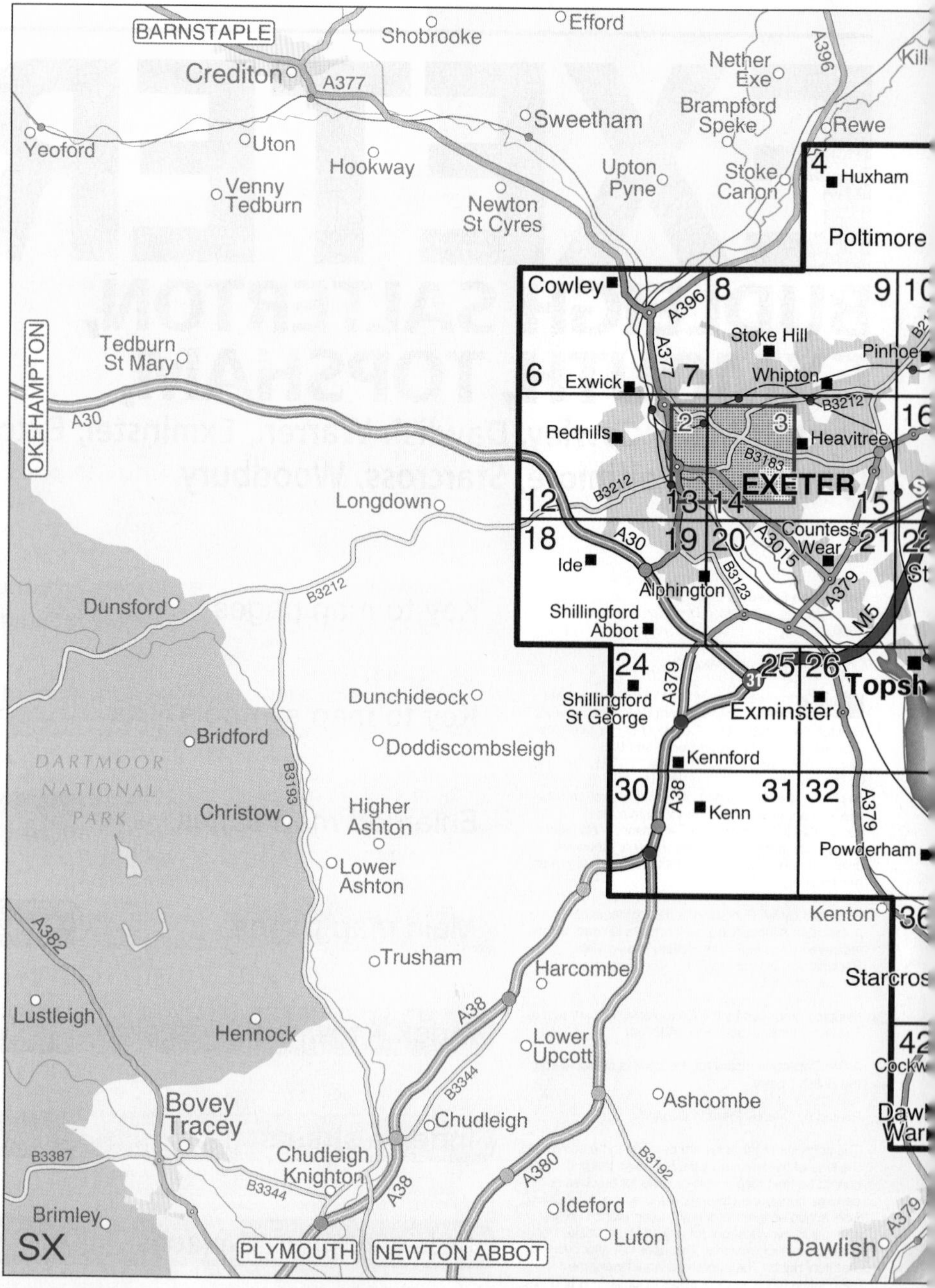
BARNSTAPLE
Efford
Shobrooke
Crediton
A377
Nether Exe
A396
Kill
Brampford Speke
Rewe
Sweetham
Yeoford
Uton
Hookway
Upton Pyne
Stoke Canon
4
Huxham
Venny Tedburn
Newton St Cyres
Poltimore
Cowley
8
9
A396
Stoke Hill
Pinhoe
OKEHAMPTON
Tedburn St Mary
A377
6
Exwick
7
Whipton
B3212
A30
Redhills
2
3
Heavitree
B3183
EXETER
12
B3212
13
14
15
Longdown
18
A30
19
20
Countess Wear
21
Ide
A3015
B3123
A379
Alphington
Dunsford
B3212
Shillingford Abbot
M5
24
A379
25
26
Topsh
Shillingford St George
Exminster
Dunchideock
Bridford
Doddiscombsleigh
Kennford
DARTMOOR NATIONAL PARK
B3193
30
A38
31
32
Kenn
A379
Christow
Higher Ashton
Powderham
Lower Ashton
Kenton
A382
Trusham
Starcros
Harcombe
Lustleigh
A38
Hennock
Lower Upcott
42
Cockw
B3344
Ashcombe
Bovey Tracey
Chudleigh
Dawl
B3387
Chudleigh Knighton
A380
B3192
B3344
A38
Ideford
A379
Brimley
SX
PLYMOUTH
NEWTON ABBOT
Luton
Dawlish

Scale of enlarged map pages 1:10,000 6.3 inches to 1 mile

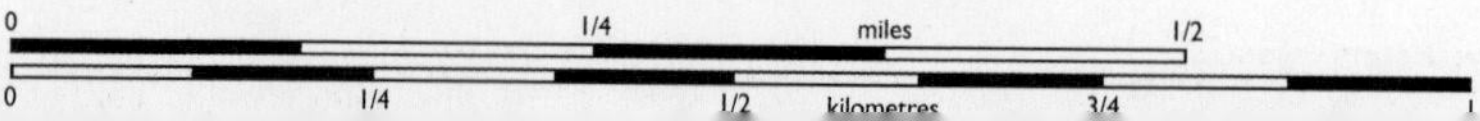
0
1/4
miles
1/2
0
1/4
1/2
kilometres
3/4
1

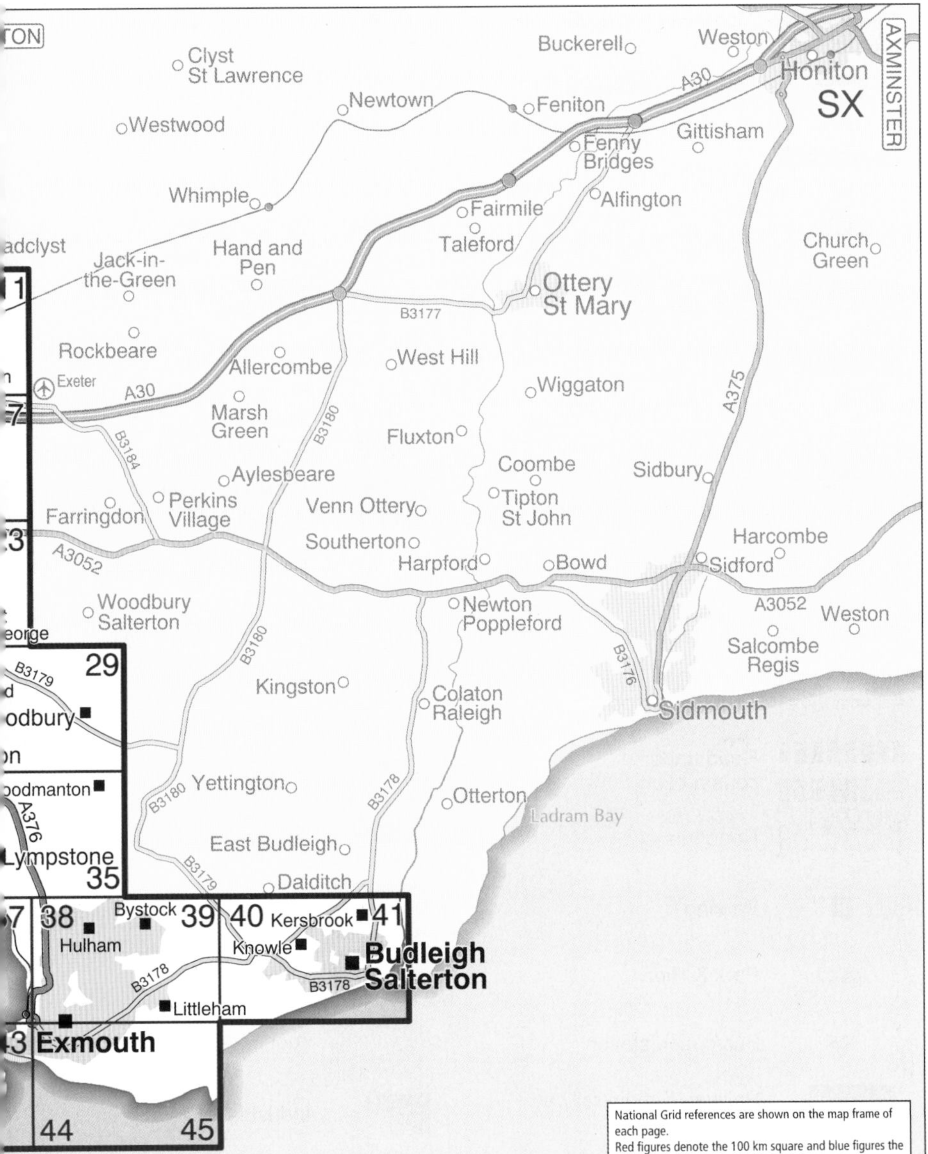

AXMINSTER
Buckerell
Weston
Honiton
SX
A30
Clyst St Lawrence
Newtown
Feniton
Westwood
Gittisham
Fenny Bridges
Alfington
Whimple
Fairmile
Taleford
Church Green
Jack-in-the-Green
Hand and Pen
Ottery St Mary
B3177
Rockbeare
Allercombe
West Hill
Exeter
Wiggaton
A375
Marsh Green
B3180
Fluxton
B3184
Coombe
Sidbury
Aylesbeare
Perkins Village
Farringdon
Venn Ottery
Tipton St John
Harcombe
Southerton
A3052
Harpford
Bowd
Sidford
Newton Poppleford
A3052
Weston
Woodbury Salterton
Salcombe Regis
29
B3179
B3176
Kingston
Colaton Raleigh
Sidmouth
Yettington
B3178
Otterton
Ladram Bay
A376
Lympstone
35
East Budleigh
Dalditch
38
Bystock
39
40
Kersbrook
41
Hulham
Knowle
Budleigh Salterton
B3178
Littleham
Exmouth
44
45

National Grid references are shown on the map frame of each page.
Red figures denote the 100 km square and blue figures the 1 km square.
Example, page 7 :
Cowley Bridge Road Business Park 291 094

The reference can also be written using the National Grid two-letter prefix shown on this page, where 2 and 0 are replaced by SX to give SX9194.

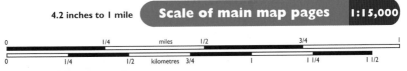

4.2 inches to 1 mile

Scale of main map pages **1:15,000**

miles	0	1/4	1/2	3/4	1		
kilometres	0	1/4	1/2	3/4	1	1 1/4	1 1/2

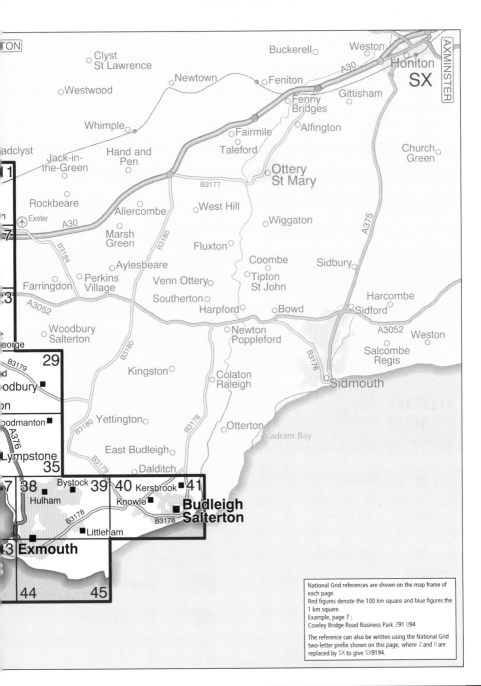

- Junction 9 — Motorway & junction
- Services — Motorway service area
- Primary road single/dual carriageway
- Services — Primary road service area
- A road single/dual carriageway
- B road single/dual carriageway
- Other road single/dual carriageway
- Minor/private road, access may be restricted
- One-way street
- Pedestrian area
- Track or footpath
- Road under construction
- Road tunnel
- P — Parking
- P+ — Park & Ride
- Bus/coach station
- Railway & main railway station
- Railway & minor railway station
- Underground station
- Light railway & station
- Preserved private railway

- LC — Level crossing
- Tramway
- Ferry route
- Airport runway
- County, administrative boundary
- Mounds
- 17 — Page continuation 1:15,000
- 3 — Page continuation to enlarged scale 1:10,000
- River/canal, lake, pier
- Aqueduct, lock, weir
- 465 Winter Hill — Peak (with height in metres)
- Beach
- Woodland
- Park
- Cemetery
- Built-up area
- Industrial building
- Leisure building
- Retail building
- Other building

City wall

A&E Hospital with 24-hour A&E department

PO Post Office

Public library

Tourist Information Centre

Seasonal Tourist Information Centre

Petrol station, 24 hour
Major suppliers only

Church/chapel

Public toilets

Toilet with disabled facilities

PH Public house
AA recommended

Restaurant
AA inspected

Madeira Hotel — Hotel
AA inspected

Theatre or performing arts centre

Cinema

Golf course

Camping
AA inspected

Caravan site
AA inspected

Camping & caravan site
AA inspected

Theme park

Abbey, cathedral or priory

Castle

Historic house or building

Wakehurst Place NT — National Trust property

Museum or art gallery

Roman antiquity

Ancient site, battlefield or monument

Industrial interest

Garden

Garden Centre
Garden Centre Association Member

Garden Centre
Wyevale Garden Centre

Arboretum

Farm or animal centre

Zoological or wildlife collection

Bird collection

Nature reserve

Aquarium

Visitor or heritage centre

Country park

Cave

Windmill

Distillery, brewery or vineyard

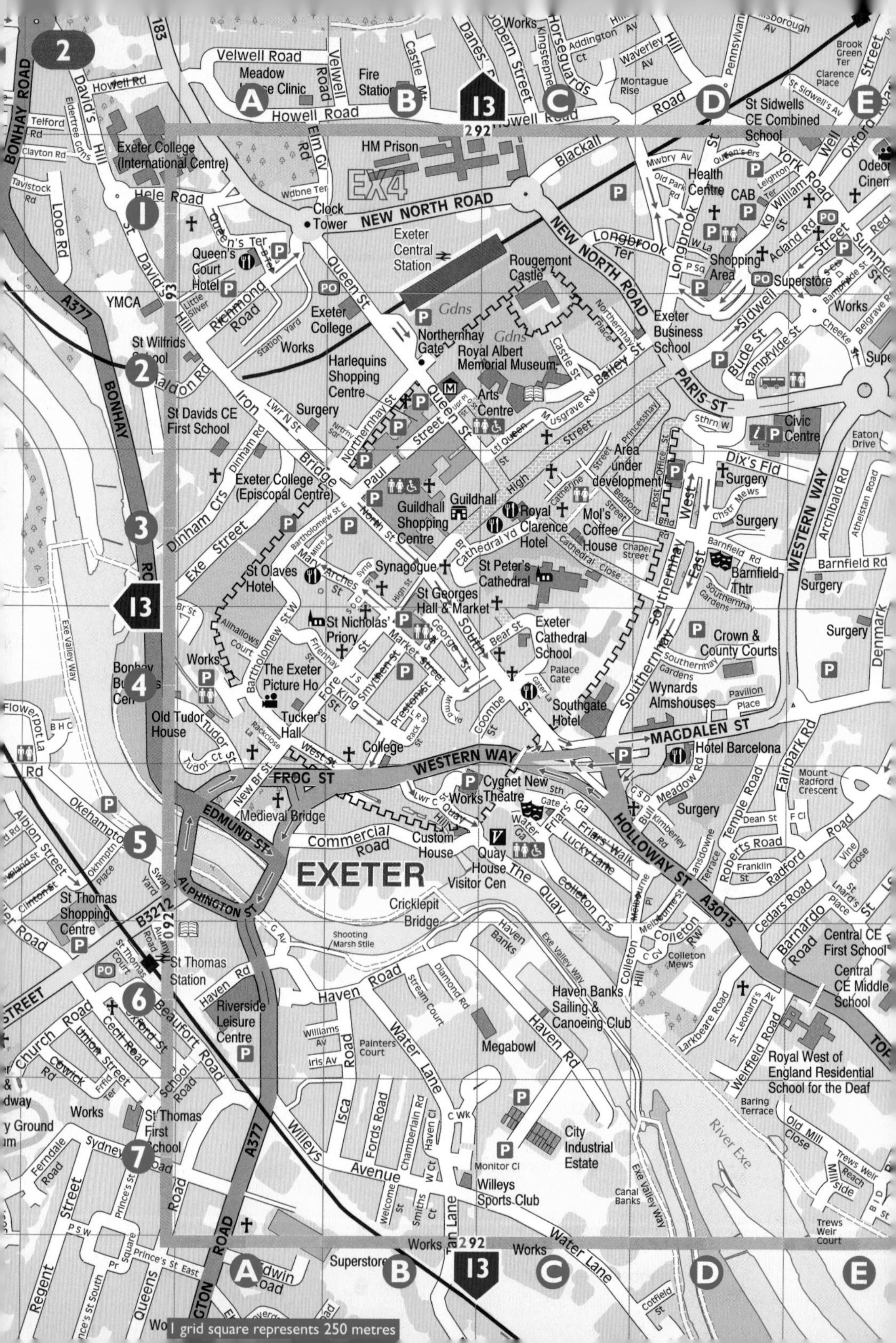

1 grid square represents 250 metres

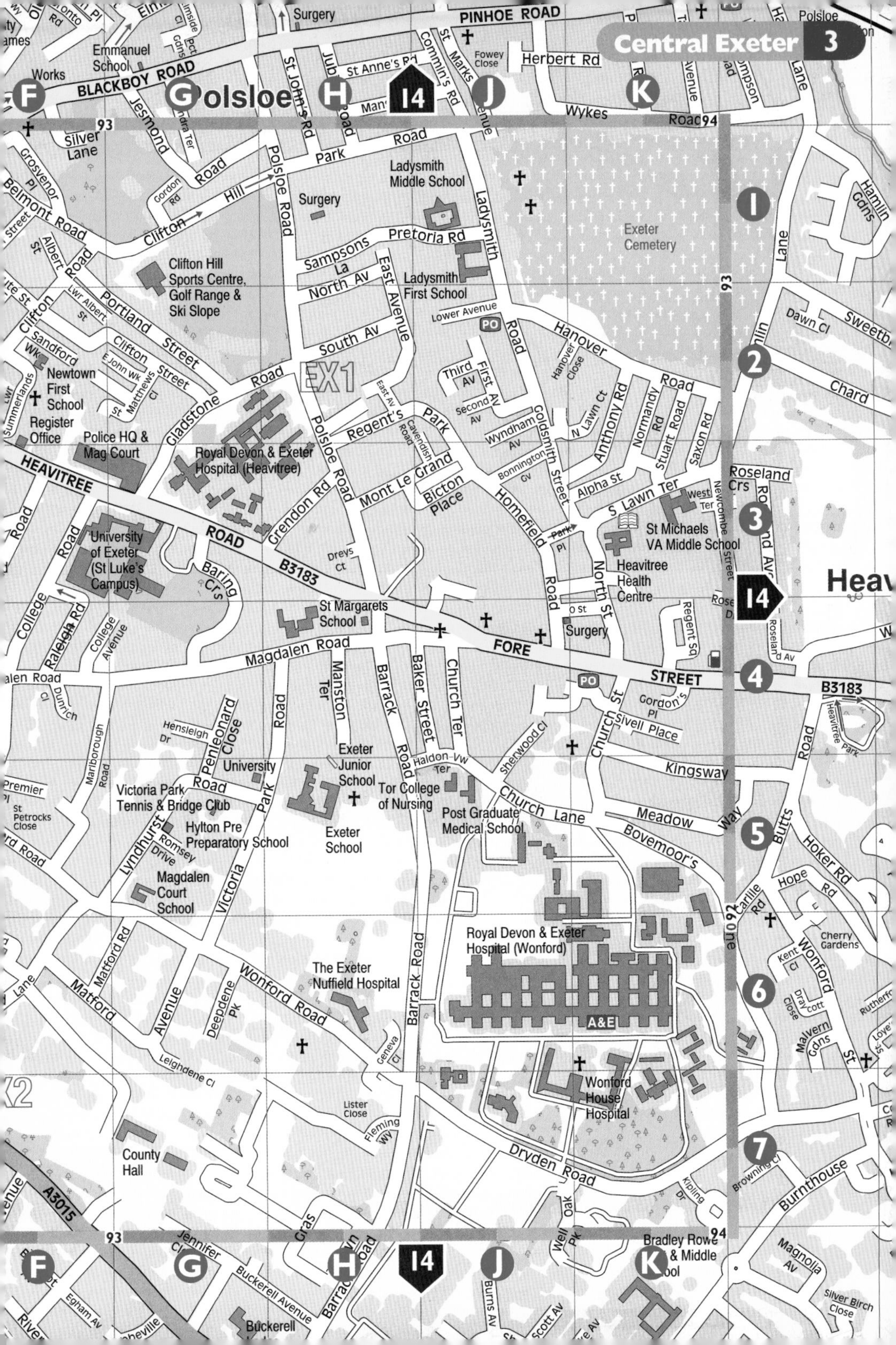
PINHOE ROAD
BLACKBOY ROAD
Polsloe
Surgery
Emmanuel School
Works
Jesmond
St Anne's Rd
Commin's Rd
St Marks Avenue
Fowey Close
Herbert Rd
Wykes Road
Silver Lane
Grosvenor Pl
Belmont Road
Gordon Rd
Clifton Hill
Polsloe Road
Park Road
Ladysmith Middle School
Ladysmith Road
Surgery
Pretoria Rd
Sampsons La
North Av
East Avenue
Ladysmith First School
Exeter Cemetery
Hamlin Gdns
Hamlin Lane
Dawn Cl
Sweetbriar
Chard
Clifton Hill Sports Centre, Golf Range & Ski Slope
Albert St
Portland Street
Lwr Albert St
Clifton St
Sandford Wk
Clifton Street
E John Wk
St Matthews Cl
Newtown First School
Summerlands
Register Office
Police HQ & Mag Court
Lower Avenue
PO
South Av
EX1
Gladstone Road
Third Av
First Av
Second Av
Hanover Road
Hanover Close
N Lawn Ct
Anthony Rd
Normandy Rd
Stuart Road
Saxon Rd
Royal Devon & Exeter Hospital (Heavitree)
Regent's Park
East Av
Cavendish Road
Wyndham Av
Goldsmith Street
Bonnington Gv
Alpha St
S Lawn Ter
West Ter
Roseland Crs
Roseland Av
HEAVITREE ROAD
Grendon Rd
Mont Le Grand
Bicton Place
Homefield Road
Park Pl
St Michaels VA Middle School
Newcombe Street
University of Exeter (St Luke's Campus)
Baring Crs
B3183
Dreys Ct
North St
Heavitree Health Centre
Heavitree
St Margarets School
O St
Surgery
Regent Sq
Rose Dr
College Road
Raleigh Rd
College Avenue
Magdalen Road
FORE STREET
PO
Gordon's Pl
Sivell Place
B3183
Heavitree Park
Magdalen Road
Dunrich Cl
Marlborough Road
Hensleigh Dr
Penleonard Close
Manston Ter
Barrack Road
Baker Street
Church Ter
Sherwood Cl
Church St
Kingsway
Premier Pl
St Petrocks Close
University
Exeter Junior School
Haldon-Vw Ter
Victoria Park Road
Victoria Park Tennis & Bridge Club
Tor College of Nursing
Post Graduate Medical School
Church Lane
Meadow Way
Bovemoor's Lane
Butts Road
Hoker Rd
Lyndhurst Road
Hylton Pre Preparatory School
Romsey Drive
Exeter School
Hope Rd
Magdalen Court School
Carlile Rd
Matford Rd
Royal Devon & Exeter Hospital (Wonford)
Cherry Gardens
Kent Cl
Wonford Road
The Exeter Nuffield Hospital
Wonford Road
Matford Lane
Avenue
Deepdene Pk
Draycott Close
Malvern Gdns
Wonford St
A&E
Rutherford
Geneva Cl
Leighdene Cl
Wonford House Hospital
Lister Close
Fleming Wy
County Hall
Dryden Road
Browning Cl
Burnthouse Lane
Kipling Dr
Well Oak Pk
A3015
Jennifer Cl
Buckerell Avenue
Barrack Road
Burns Av
Scott Av
Bradley Rowe First & Middle School
Magnolia Av
Silver Birch Close
Egham Av
Buckerell
I4
93
94
92
F G H J K
1 2 3 4 5 6 7

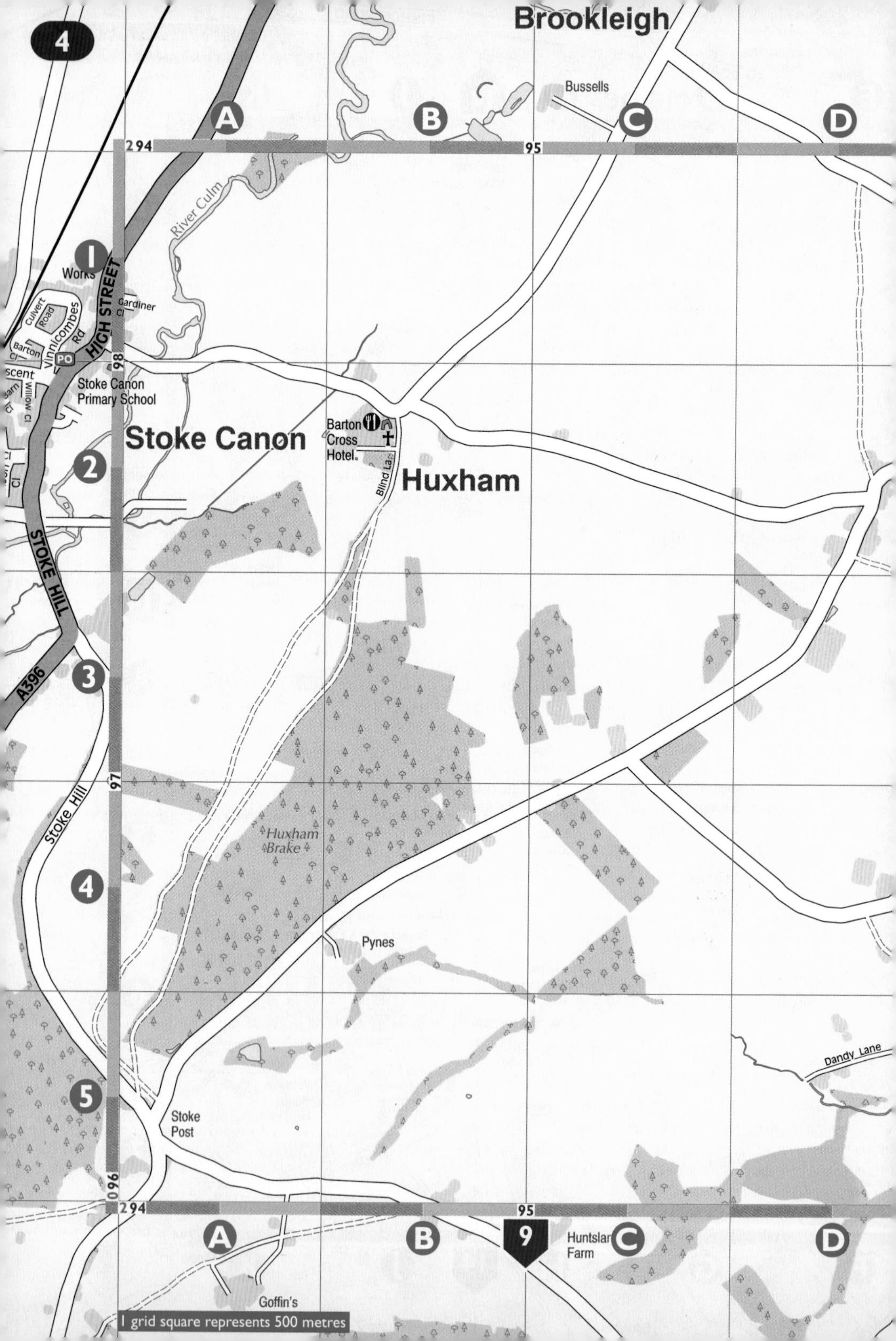
Brookleigh
Bussells
A
B
C
D
294
95
River Culm
1
Works
HIGH STREET
Cardiner Cl
Culvert Road
Vinnicombes Rd
Barton Cl
PO
98
Stoke Canon Primary School
Willow Cl
Stoke Canon
Barton Cross Hotel
Blind La
Huxham
2
STOKE HILL
3
A396
97
Stoke Hill
Huxham Brake
4
Pynes
Dandy Lane
5
Stoke Post
096
9
Huntsla Farm
Goffin's

1 grid square represents 500 metres

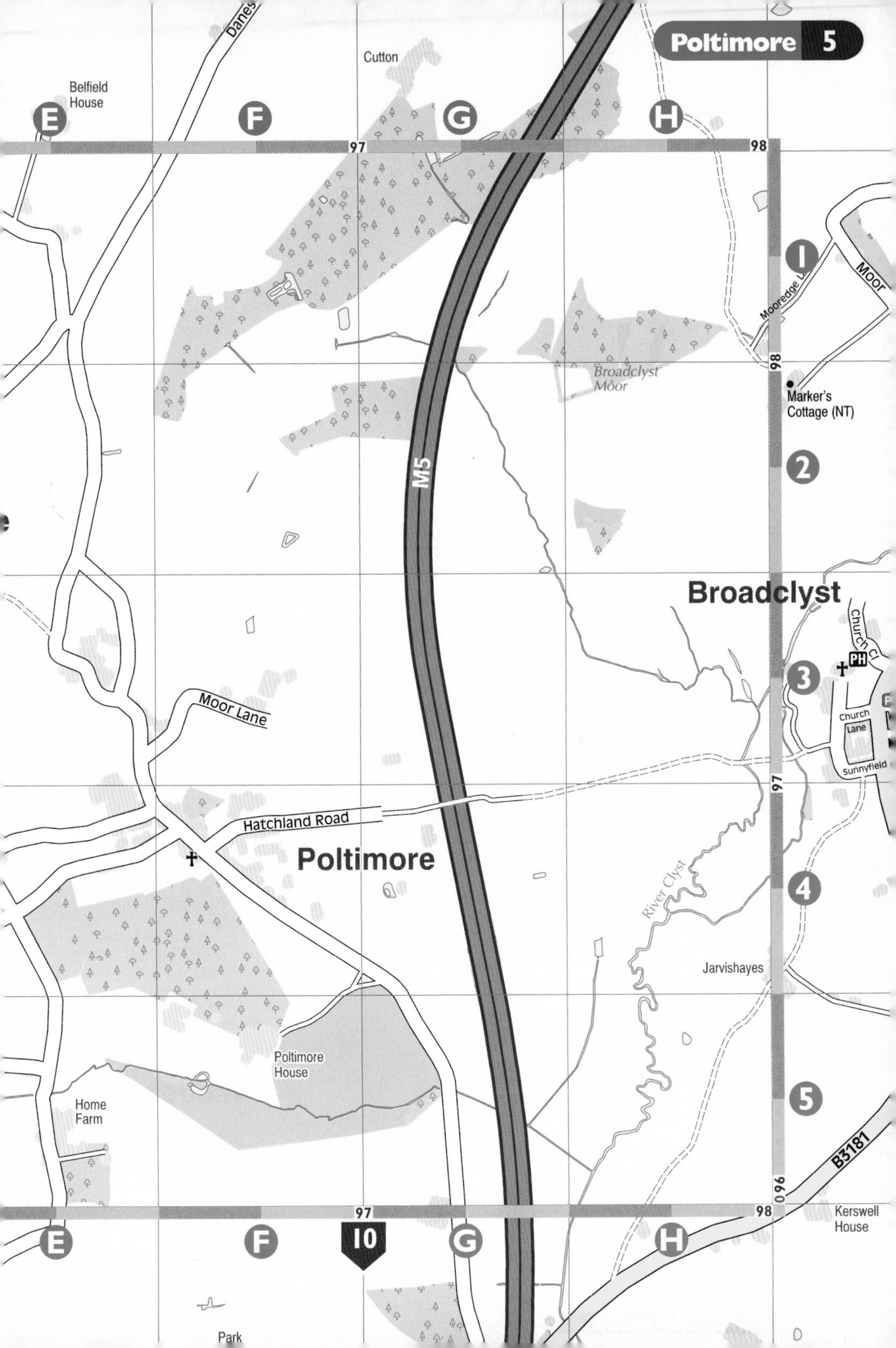
Danes
Cutton
Belfield House
E
F
G
H
97
98
I
Mooredge La
Moor
Broadclyst Moor
Marker's Cottage (NT)
M5
2
Broadclyst
Church Cl
PH
3
Church Lane
Sunnyfield
Moor Lane
Hatchland Road
Poltimore
River Clyst
4
Jarvishayes
Poltimore House
Home Farm
5
B3181
96
Kerswell House
10
Park

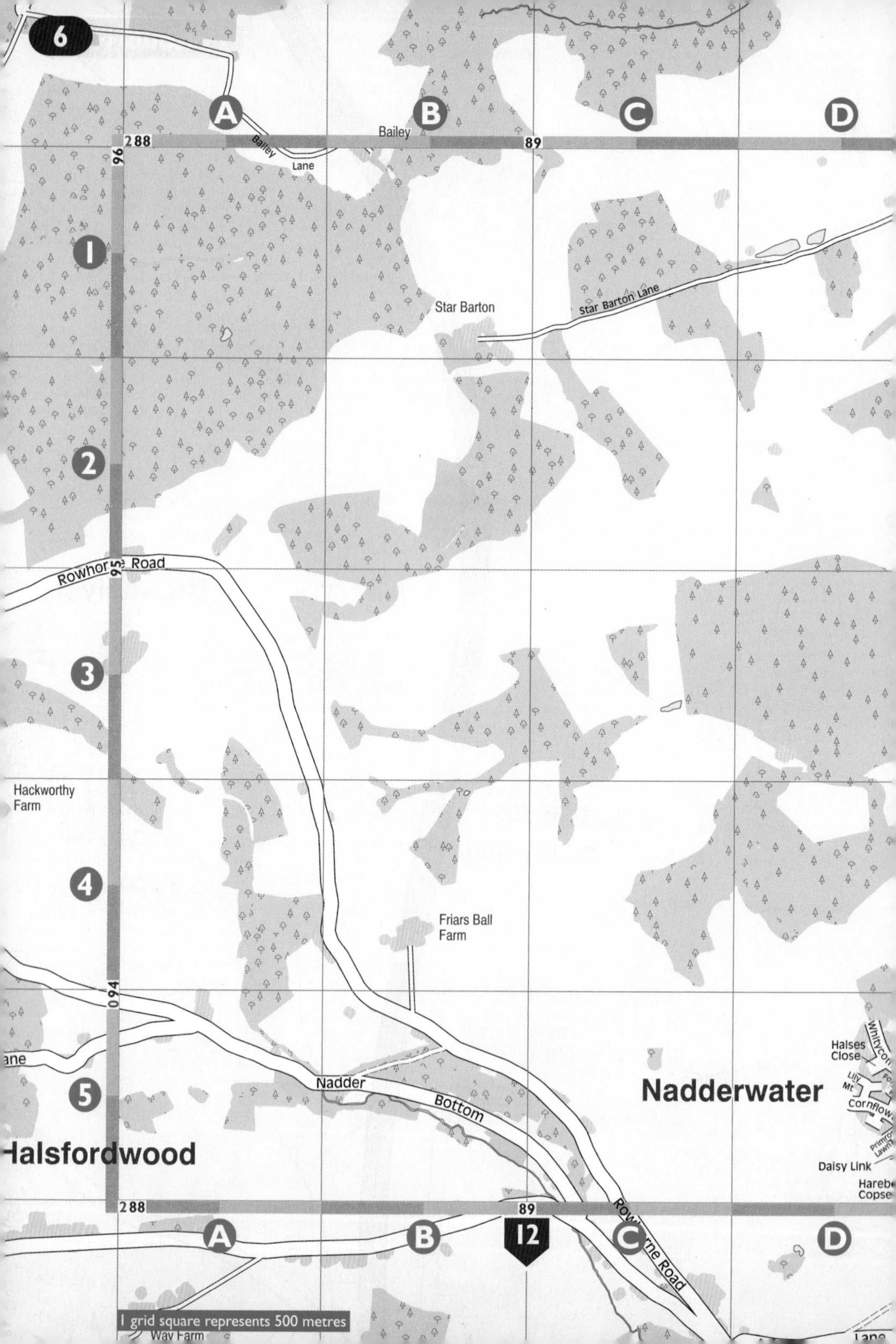
6
A
B
C
D
288
89
96
Bailey
Bailey
Lane
1
Star Barton
Star Barton Lane
2
Rowhorne Road
95
3
Hackworthy
Farm
4
Friars Ball
Farm
094
ane
5
Nadder
Bottom
Halsfordwood
Nadderwater
Halses
Close
Lily
Mt
Daisy Link
288
89
A
B
12
C
D
Rowhorne Road
1 grid square represents 500 metres
Way Farm

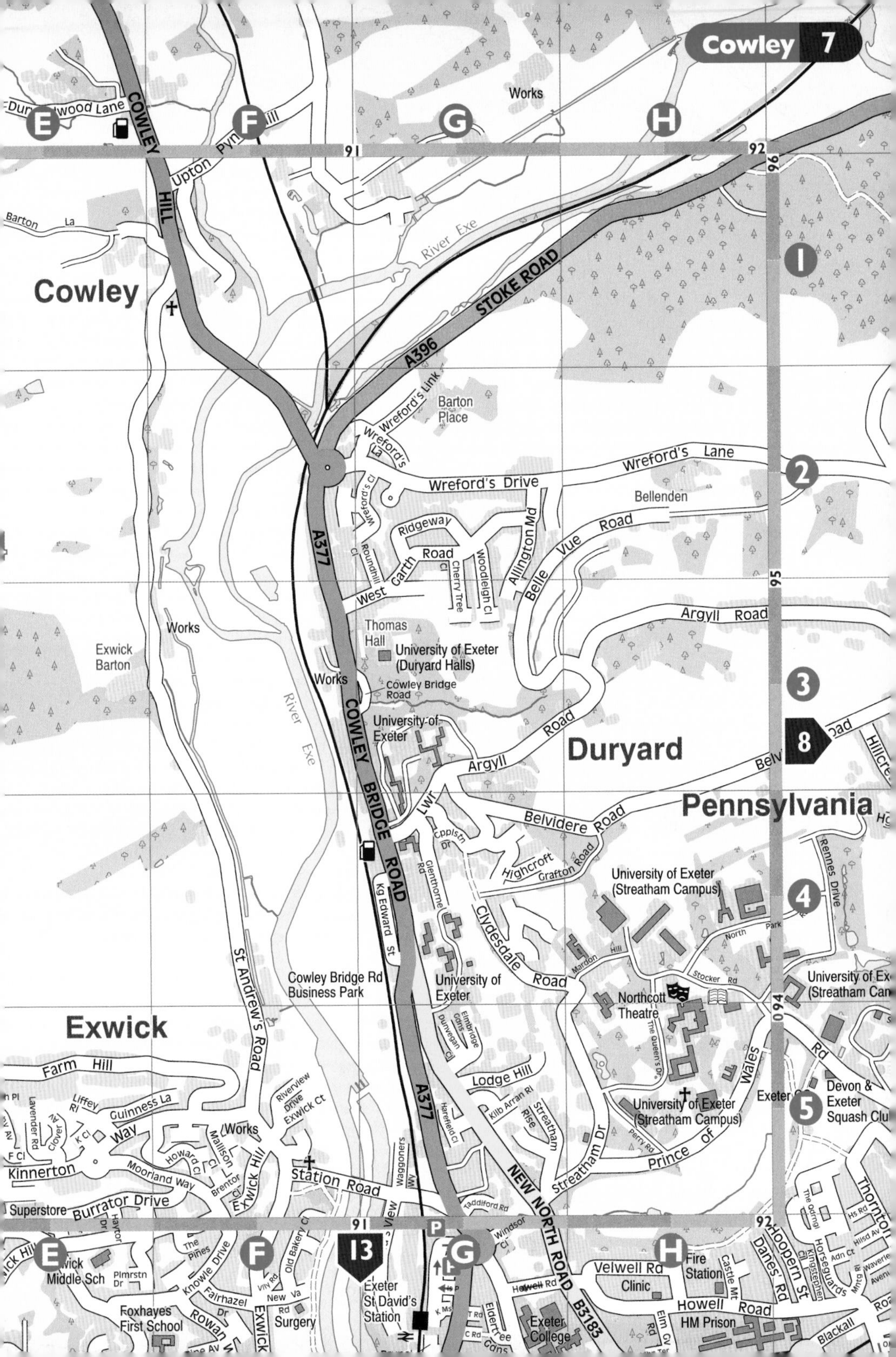
Cowley
Durward Lane
COWLEY HILL
Upton Pyne Hill
Barton La
Works
River Exe
STOKE ROAD
A396
Wreford's Link
Barton Place
Wreford's La
Wreford's Cl
Wreford's Drive
Wreford's Lane
Bellenden
Belle Vue Road
Ridgeway
Roundhill Cl
West Garth Road
Cherry Tree Cl
Woodleigh Cl
Allington Md
Argyll Road
A377
Thomas Hall
University of Exeter (Duryard Halls)
Cowley Bridge Road
Exwick Barton
University of Exeter
Duryard
Pennsylvania
Belvidere Road
COWLEY BRIDGE ROAD
Lwr
Cpplstn Dr
Glenthorne Rd
Highcroft
Grafton Road
University of Exeter (Streatham Campus)
Rennes Drive
North Park Rd
Kg Edward St
Clydesdale Road
Mardon Hill
Stocker Rd
Northcott Theatre
University of Exeter (Streatham Campus)
Cowley Bridge Rd Business Park
St Andrew's Road
Exwick
Farm Hill
Dunvegan Gdns
Elmbridge Gdns
The Queen's Dr
Lodge Hill
Liffey Ri
Guinness La
Lavender Rd
Clover Av
K Cl
F Cl
Way
Kinnerton
Moorland Way
Howard Cl
Mallison Cl
Brentor Cl
Works
Riverview Drive
Exwick Ct
Exwick Hill
Station Road
Waggoners Wy
Harefield Cl
Kilb Arran Rl
Streatham Rise
Perry Rd
Streatham Dr
Prince of Wales Rd
Exeter
Devon & Exeter Squash Club
Superstore
Burrator Drive
Haytor Dr
Taddiford Rd
NEW NORTH ROAD
Thornton
The Pines
Knowle Drive
Old Bakery Cl
View
Windsor Cl
Hs Rd
Hlsd Av
Adn Ct
Waverley Avenue
Exwick Middle Sch
Plmrstn Dr
Fairhazel Dr
Vlly Rd
New Va Rd
Exeter St David's Station
Velwell Rd
Howell Rd
Clinic
Fire Station
Castle Mt
Hoopern St
Danes' Rd
Kingstephen Cl
Horseguards
Mntg Rl
Foxhayes First School
Rowan Way
EXWICK
Surgery
Elderfree Gdns
Exeter College
B3183
Elm Gv Rd
Howell Road
HM Prison
Blackall Rd
91
92
96
95
094
E
F
G
H
1
2
3
4
5
8
13
P

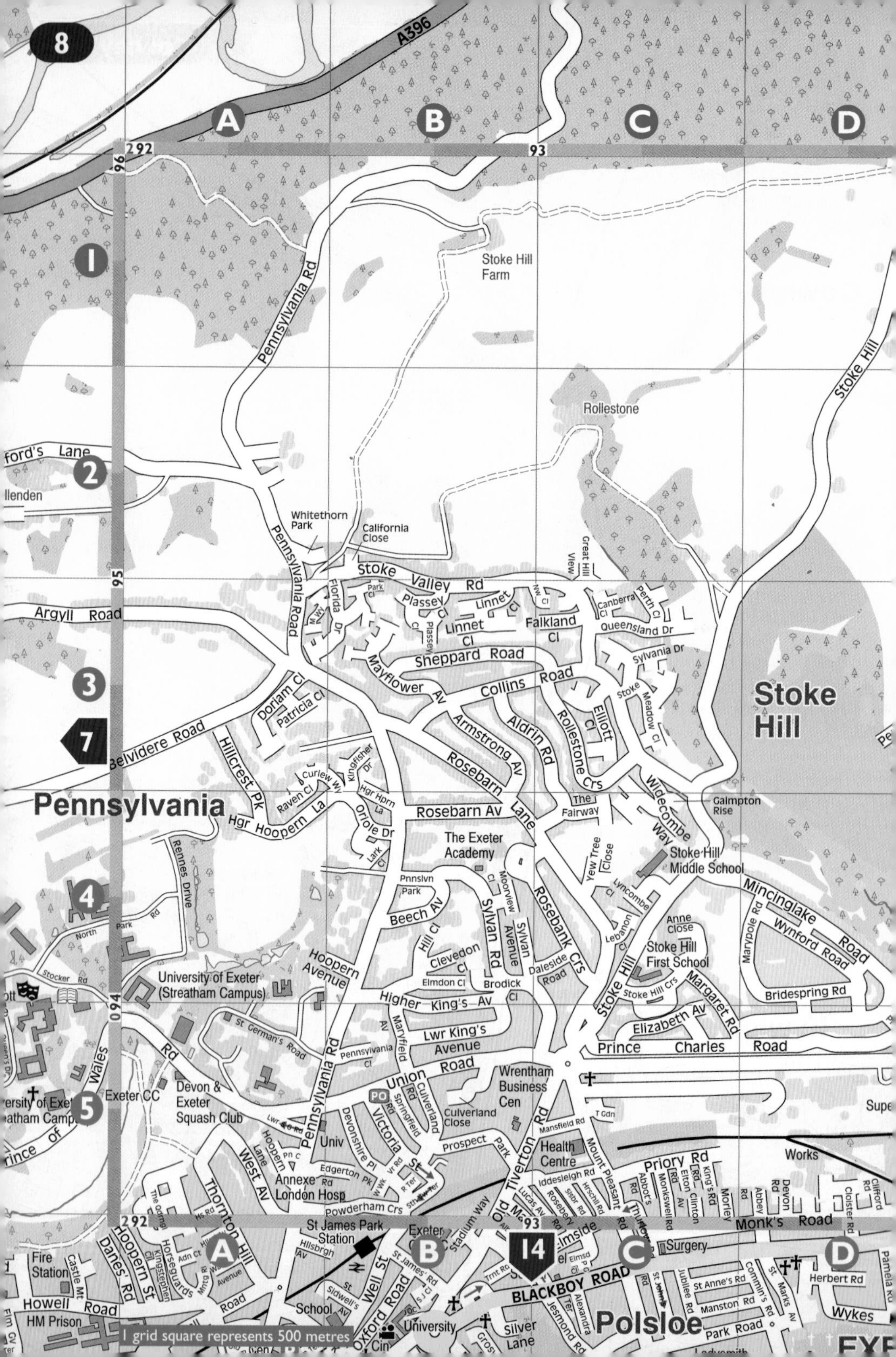

8
A396
A
B
C
D
292
93
96
1
Pennsylvania Rd
Stoke Hill Farm
Rollestone
Stoke Hill
ford's Lane
2
llenden
Whitethorn Park
California Close
Pennsylvania Road
Great Hill View
Stoke Valley Rd
95
Argyll Road
Florida Dr
Park Cl
Plassey Cl
Plassey Cl
Linnet Cl
Linnet Cl
Nw Cl
Falkland Cl
Canberra Cl
Perth Cl
Queensland Dr
Sylvania Dr
Sheppard Road
Mayflower Av
Collins Road
Stoke Meadow Cl
Elliott Cl
Rollestone Crs
Aldrin Rd
Armstrong Av
3
Doriam Cl
Patricia Cl
Stoke Hill
7
Belvidere Road
Hillcrest Pk
Kingfisher Dr
Curlew Wy
Raven Cl
Hgr Hprn La
Rosebarn Lane
Widecombe Way
Galmpton Rise
The Fairway
Pennsylvania
Hgr Hoopern La
Oriole Dr
Rosebarn Av
Lark Cl
The Exeter Academy
Yew Tree Close
Stoke Hill Middle School
Rennes Drive
Pnnslvn Park
Moorview Cl
Rosebank Crs
Lyncombe
Mincinglake Road
4
North Park Rd
Beech Av
Hill Cl
Sylvan Rd
Sylvan Avenue
Lebanon Cl
Anne Close
Marypole Rd
Wynford Road
Clevedon Cl
Stoke Hill First School
Stocker Rd
University of Exeter (Streatham Campus)
Hoopern Avenue
Elmdon Cl
Brodick Cl
Daleside Road
Stoke Hill
Stoke Hill Crs
Margaret Rd
Bridespring Rd
094
Higher King's Av
Elizabeth Av
St German's Road
Maryfield Av
Lwr King's Avenue
Prince Charles Road
Wales
Rd
Pennsylvania Rd
Pennsylvania Cl
Union Road
Wrentham Business Cen
Devon & Exeter Squash Club
Culverland Rd
Exeter CC
5
rince of
PO
Springfield Rd
Victoria
Culverland Close
Tiverton Rd
Mansfield Rd
T Gdn
Supe
Lwr Hoopern Lane
West Av
Pn C
Devonshire Pl
Univ
Prospect Park
Health Centre
Mount Pleasant Rd
Works
Thornton Hill
Edgerton Pk Rd
Vr Rd
St
Priory Rd
Abbot's Rd
Monkswell Rd
Elton Rd
Clinton Av
Rd
King's Rd
Morley Rd
Abbey Rd
Devon Rd
Cloister Rd
Clifford Rd
Annexe London Hosp
Iddesleigh Rd
Lucas Av
Rosebery Rd
Sispr Rd
Hrschll Rd
Powderham Crs
Horseguards
Hs Rd
Stadium Way
Old Tiverton Rd
292
St James Park Station
Exeter
93
Monk's Road
Hoopern St
Kingsstephen
Adn Ct
Hllsbrgh Av
Elmside
Surgery
Fire Station
Castle Mt
Danes' Rd
A
B
14
C
D
Well St
St James' Rd
Elmsd Cl
St Anne's Rd
Commin's Rd
St Marks Av
Herbert Rd
Pamela Rd
Avenue
Sidwell's Av
BLACKBOY ROAD
Jubilee Rd
Howell Road
Road
School
Oxford Road
Manston Rd
Wykes
HM Prison
Jesmond Rd
Alexandra Ter
Polsloe
Park Road
University
Silver Lane
1 grid square represents 500 metres
Cin

Stoke Post
E
F
4
G
H
95
96
Huntsland Farm
Goffin's Farm
I
2
Cheynegate Lane
Church Lane
Park Lane
Bindon Road
Broadparks
Church Hill
3
10
Danesway
Celia Crs
Cottey Crs
Chancellor's Way
Savoy Hl
Iolanthe Drive
Lancelot Road
Tristan Cl
Pellinore Rd
Spruce Cl
Tamarisk Cl
Juniper Cl
Meadow Dr
Pinwood
Whitebeam Close
Ilex Cl
Fox Road
Central Av
Brookside Crs
Pinwood La
Beacon Lane
Beacon Heath
Harrington Lane
Cheyne Ri
Matthews Ct
Pulling Rd
Puckridge Rd
Bourn Ri
Bickleigh Cl
Harrington Dr
Reynolds Close
Bradfield Road
De La Rue Way
Chancel Lane
Lands Road
Wilcocks Road
Pinhoe CE Combined School
Lower Harrington Lane
Harrington Gdns
Oak Close
4
St James High School
Galahad Cl
Camelot Cl
Beacon La
Northbrook Cl
Arena Pk
Arena Park
Works
Pinbrook Industrial Estate
St James Sports Centre
Excalibur Cl
Guinevere Wy
Fouracre Cl
Tor Cl
Willowbrook School
Roundtable Meet
Summer Lane
Surgery
Bettys Md
Atkinson Cl
Atkinson Unit
Venny Br
Pinhoe Station
Hummingbird Close
Broadleigh Close
Monkerton
Bazley Square
PINHOE ROAD
B3181
094
Walpole Cl
Bernadette Cl
Orwill Ga
Ivy Sq
Prs Av
Kingsley Avenue
Masefield Rd
Summerway
Sheridan Road
Warwick Wy
Exhibition Way
Pinbrook Road
Stratford Avenue
Grenville Avenue
Trading Estate
Pilton La
Austen Cl
Conrad Av
Wallace Avenue
Summerway Middle School
Thackeray Road
The Mede
Woolsery Grove
Woolsery Close
Woolsery Avenue
Kennerley Avenue
Westbrook Cl
Summer Cl
Whipton
Hart's Lane
5
Superstore
Monkerton
Bennett Sq
Widgery Road
Widgery Rd
Rdlnds Cl
Whipton Rd
Beacon Lane
Whipton Village Rd
PO
Surg
B3212 PINHOE ROAD
Fairfield Avenue
Hospital La
Honeylands Hospital for Children
Whipton Barton First School
Lamacraft Dr
Brook Close
Crescent
Lids Crt
Whipton Hospital
Hollow Lane
Ellen Special
Honeylands Dr
Polsloe Bridge Station
Honeylands Wy
Vranch House School
Staddon Cl
Whipton Barton Middle Sch
Bonville Cl
Hill Lane Road
15
Whipton
Lloyds
Alford Crs
Hillyfield Rd
Barton Road
Durham Close
Barton Cl
Hill
Greenpark Av
Wood Rd
Hamlin
Clifford
Headland
EX1

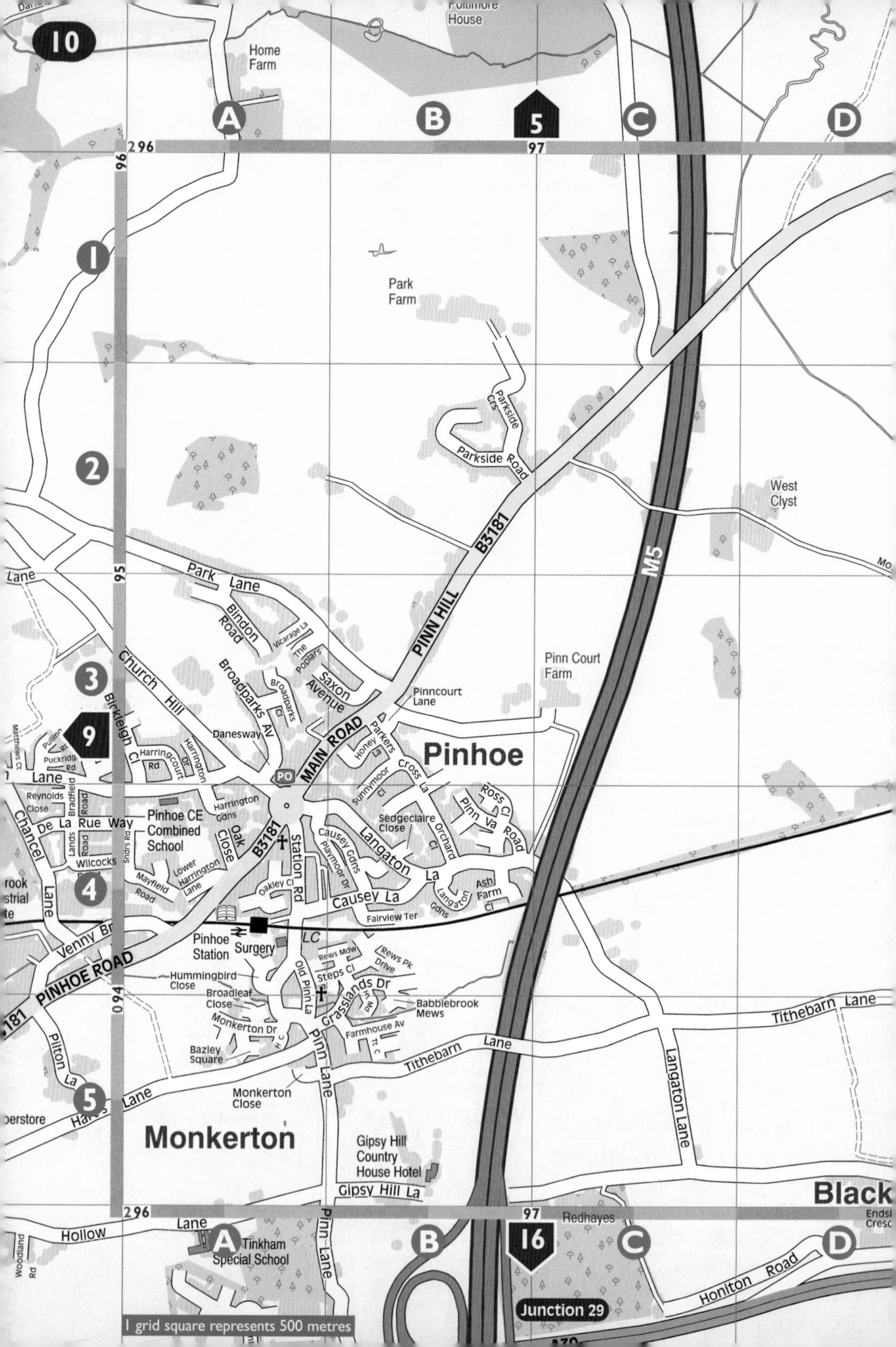
10
Poltimore House
Home Farm
A
B
5
C
D
296
97
96
95
094
1
2
3
4
5
Park Farm
Parkside Crs
Parkside Road
West Clyst
B3181
PINN HILL
M5
Park Lane
Lane
Bindon Road
Vicarage La
The Poplars
Saxon Avenue
Broadparks Av
Broadparks Cl
Church Hill
Bickleigh Cl
Danesway
Pinn Court Farm
Pinncourt Lane
MAIN ROAD
Parkers
Honey La
Pinhoe
9
Pulling Rd
Puckridge Rd
Matthews Ct
Harringcourt Rd
Harrington Dr
Harrington Gdns
PO
Sunnymoor Cl
Cross La
Ross Cl
Pinn Va Road
Orchard Cl
Sedgeclaire Close
Lane
Reynolds Close
Bradfield Road
De La Rue Way
Lands Road
Pinhoe CE Combined School
Oak Close
Station Rd
Causey Gdns
Playmoor Dr
Langaton La
Ash Farm Cl
Chancel Lane
Wilcocks Rd
Sndrs Rd
Lower Harrington Lane
Mayfield Road
Oakley Cl
Causey La
Langaton Gdns
Fairview Ter
Venny Br
Pinhoe Station
Surgery
LC
Rews Mdw
Rews Pk Drive
PINHOE ROAD
Hummingbird Close
Steps Cl
Old Pinn La
Grasslands Dr
Broadleaf Close
Babblebrook Mews
Monkerton Dr
H C
Farmhouse Av
Tr C
Tithebarn Lane
Bazley Square
Pinn Lane
Langaton Lane
Pilton La
Monkerton Close
Harts Lane
Monkerton
Gipsy Hill Country House Hotel
Gipsy Hill La
Black
Hollow Lane
Tinkham Special School
Woodland Rd
Redhayes
Endsleigh Cresc
16
Honiton Road
Junction 29
1 grid square represents 500 metres

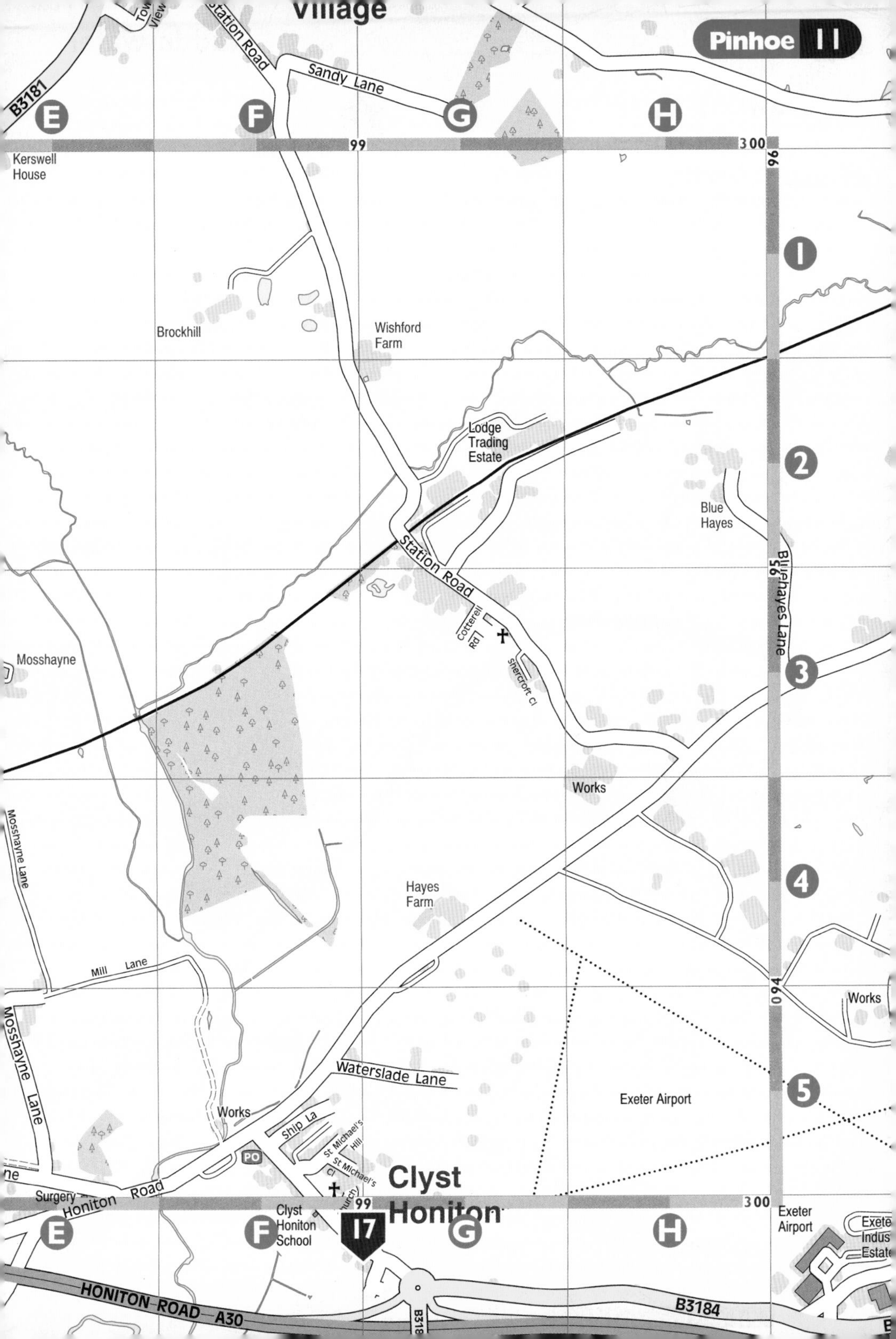
Village
Station Road
Sandy Lane
B3181
E
F
G
H
99
300
96
Kerswell House
I
Brockhill
Wishford Farm
Lodge Trading Estate
2
Blue Hayes
Station Road
95
Bluehayes Lane
Cotterell Rd
Shercroft Cl
Mosshayne
3
Works
Mosshayne Lane
Hayes Farm
4
Mill Lane
Mosshayne Lane
94
Works
Waterslade Lane
Exeter Airport
5
Works
Ship La
St Michael's Hill
St Michael's Cl
PO
Clyst Honiton
Surgery
Honiton Road
Clyst Honiton School
17
Exeter Airport
HONITON ROAD A30
B3184

12
Nadderwater
Halsfordwood
Nadder
Bottom
A
B
6
C
D
288
89
Rowhorne Road
Close
Lily Mt
Cornflow
Primr Lawn
Link
Hareb Copse
Way Farm
Exwick
Lane
Redhills
St Peters
Huroton House
93
Tedburn Road
Redh
Osbornes Farm
Barley Lane
Cutteridge
Lane
A30
Tedburn Road
Nadder Brook
TEDBURN ROAD A30
Eastwood
92
Westwood Lane
Westwood Lane
Tedburn Road
The Qu
Barley
Special
Black
Hat
Lane
Webby's Farm
BAKERS HILL
Pocombe Bridge
POCOMBE HILL
LONGDOWN ROAD
A30
90
288
Mark's
89
Lane
A
B
18
C
D
B3212
College Lane
Lane
1 grid square represents 500 metres
1
2
3
4
5

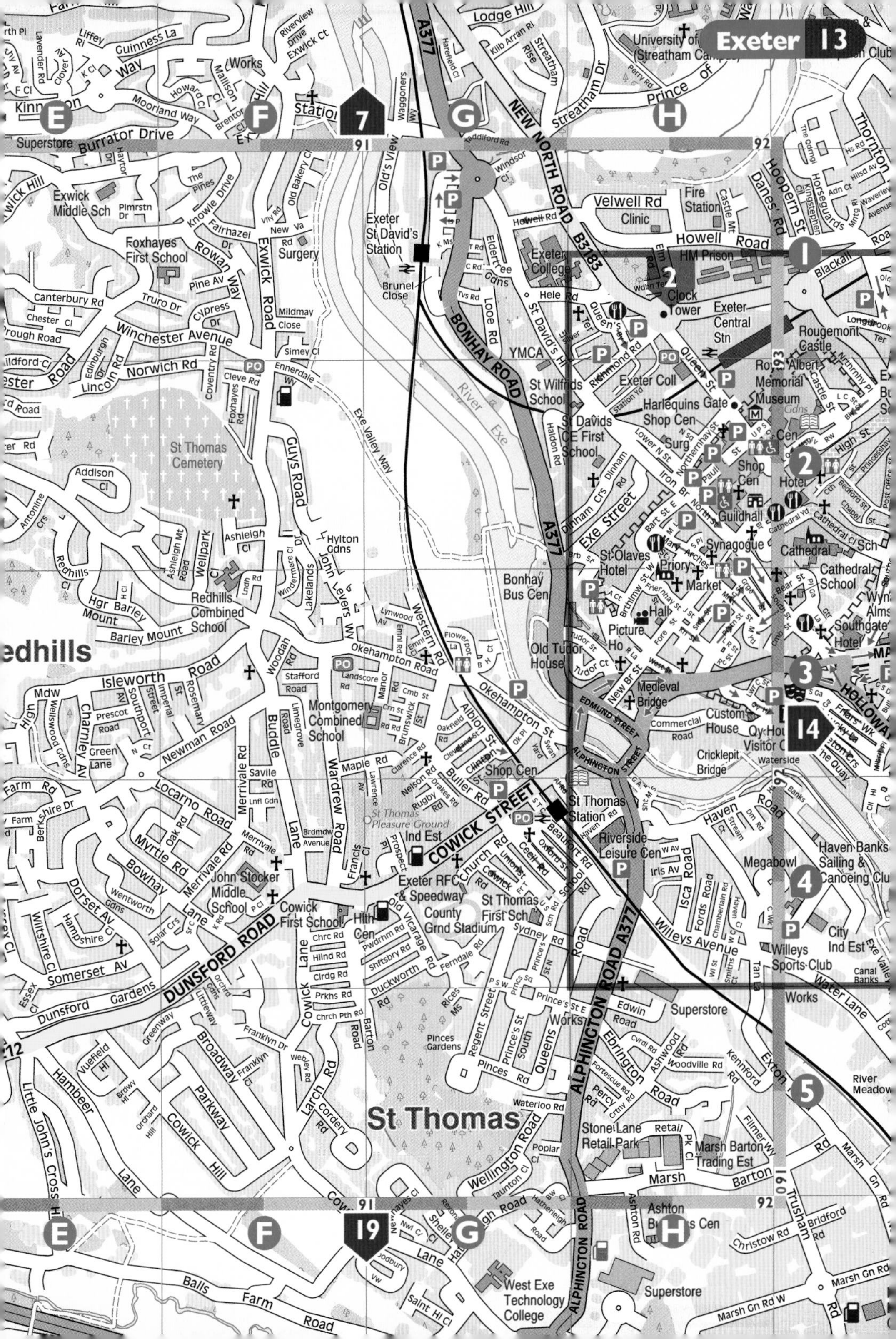
Exeter St David's Station
Exeter Central Stn
HM Prison
Clock Tower
Exeter College
Rougemont Castle
Royal Albert Memorial Museum
Harlequins Gate
Guildhall Shop Cen
Cathedral
Cathedral School
Synagogue
St Olaves Hotel
Priory
Market
Picture Ho
Old Tudor House
Medieval Bridge
Custom House
Cricklepit Bridge
Bonhay Bus Cen
St Wilfrids School
St Davids CE First School
YMCA
Exeter Coll
Velwell Rd Clinic
Fire Station
University of Exeter (Streatham Campus)
St Thomas Station
Riverside Leisure Cen
Megabowl
Haven Banks Sailing & Canoeing Club
City Ind Est
Willeys Sports Club
Superstore
Stone Lane Retail Park
Marsh Barton Trading Est
Ashton Business Cen
West Exe Technology College
St Thomas
Pinces Gardens
Exeter RFC & Speedway County Grnd Stadium
St Thomas First Sch
Cowick First School
John Stocker Middle School
Montgomery Combined School
Redhills Combined School
Redhills
St Thomas Cemetery
Foxhayes First School
Exwick Middle Sch
St Thomas Pleasure Ground
Ind Est
Hlth Cen
Surgery
Works
River Exe
Exe Valley Way
NEW NORTH ROAD B3183
BONHAY ROAD A377
COWICK STREET
DUNSFORD ROAD
ALPHINGTON ROAD A377
Okehampton Road
Isleworth Road
Exwick Road
Guys Road
Winchester Avenue
Burrator Drive
Howell Road
Exe Street
Willeys Avenue
Water Lane
Marsh Barton Road
Balls Farm Road
Cowick Hill
Cowick Lane
Buddle Lane
Wardrew Road
Haven Road
Isca Road
Ebrington Road
Wellington Road
Queens Road
Western Rd
Okehampton St
Commercial Road
Edmund Street
Alphington Street
Queen St
High St
Fore St
Holloway
Hoopern St
Streatham Dr
Prince of Wales Rd
Lodge Hill
Dunsford Gardens
Somerset Av
Locarno Road
Newman Road
Charnley Av
Barley Mount
Hambeer Lane
Little John's Cross Hill
Broadway
Parkway
Trusham Rd
Marsh Gn Rd
River Meadows
Canal Banks
A377
E F G H
1 2 3 4 5
7 14 19
91 92 93
Superstore

1 grid square represents 500 metres

Whipton
Monker
Heavitree
EX1
Summerway Middle School
Thackeray Road
B3212 PINHOE ROAD
Superstore
Woolsery Avenue
Kennerley Avenue
Widgery Road
Bennett Sq
Beacon Lane
Whipton Village Rd
Summer Cl
Mede
The
Conrad
Fairfield
Avenue
Hospital La
Honeylands Hospital for Children
Whipton Barton First School
Vranch House School
Whipton Barton Middle Sch
Honeylands Drive
Polsloe Bridge Station
Honeylands Wy
Lamacraft Dr
Staddon Cl
Bonville Cl
Hill Lane
Brookway
Lloyds Crescent
Whipton Hospital
Hillyfield Road
Whipton Barton Road
Hill Barton Cl
Hollow Lane
Greenpark Av
Woodland Rd
Ellen
Alford Crs
Clifford Cl
Headland Crs
Leypark Road
Leypark Crs
HILL BARTON ROAD
Hill Barton La
Vaughan Road
Bodley Cl
Bowring Cl
Wayside Crs
Georges Cl
Binford Cl
Hamlin Gdns
Carlyon Cl
Carlyon Gdns
Madison Avenue
Dawn Cl
Sweetbrier Lane
Chard Road
Whiteway Drive
Whipton La
Endfield Cl
Lymeborne Av
Nicholas Rd
Mulberry Close
Thorn Cl
Heather Cl
Thornpark Rise
Blackthorn Crs
Thornberry Av
Barton Hill
Russet Av
Pippin Cl
Laxton Av
Bramley Av
Ribston Av
Sargent Cl
Membury Close
Wilton Wy
Dotton Cl
Chard Stock Close
HONITON ROAD
Emperor Way
Birchy
Warwick Road
Warwick Av
Linda Cl
Quintet Cl
St Lukes High Sch
Ringswell Av
Lower Hill Barton Road
St Lawrence Crs
Surg
B3181
A3015
Greenwood Drive
Heron Road
Whipton Lane
Lonsdale Rd
Stanwey
Victor Lane
Victor St
Sycamore Cl
Sweetbrier La
Works
B3183 HONITON ROAD
SIDMOUTH ROAD
Delius Crs
Badger Close
Purcell Cl
Hardy Rd
Byron Road
Vachell Crescent
Hamilton Dr
Mallard
EAST WONFORD HL
Heavitree Park
Glenmore Rd
Avondale Rd
Mayfield Rd
Coates Road
Grainger Cl
Broadfields Road
Walton Rd
Elgar Cl
Sullivan Rd
St Peters CE Aided School
Salter's Rd
Wilford Rd
Lethbridge Rd
Loves Rd
Attwyll Av
Hope Rd
Hoker Rd
Heath Rd
Allervale Cl
Lancstr Cl
Beverley Cl
Quarry Lane
Farm Cl
Plumtree Dr
Woodwater Lane
Rifford Road
Hurst Av
Peryam Crs
Salter's Rd
Lisa Close
Wonford St
Walter Daw First School
Whitchurch Av
Carlton Rd
Quarry Park Rd
Gilbert Av
Garden Cl
Cliff Bastin Cl
Grecian Wy
Mamhead Rd
Miller Cl
Spinney Cl
Bathern Rd
Sidmouth Road
Quarry Lane
Sowton & Digby Station
Tuckfield Cl
Coronation Rd
Ivy Cl
Superstore
Wonford Sports Centre
Aspen Cl
Parkland Dr
Woodwater La
Lords Way
Campion Gdns
Buckingham Rd
Royal Cres
Crown Wy
Digby Drive
Clyst Heath
Clyst Halt Av
Knights Crs
Baxter Cl
Apple Farm Grange
Russell Way
Woodwater La
Digby Rd
Russell Wy
Couper Mdw
Silver Birch Cl
Ludwell Lane
RYDON LANE
A3015
A379
Superstore
Russell Wy
Russell Way
Southbrook School
Wendover
Old Rydon
Hill
Iron Works
9
16
21
E F G H
1 2 3 4 5
95 96 93 92 91 90

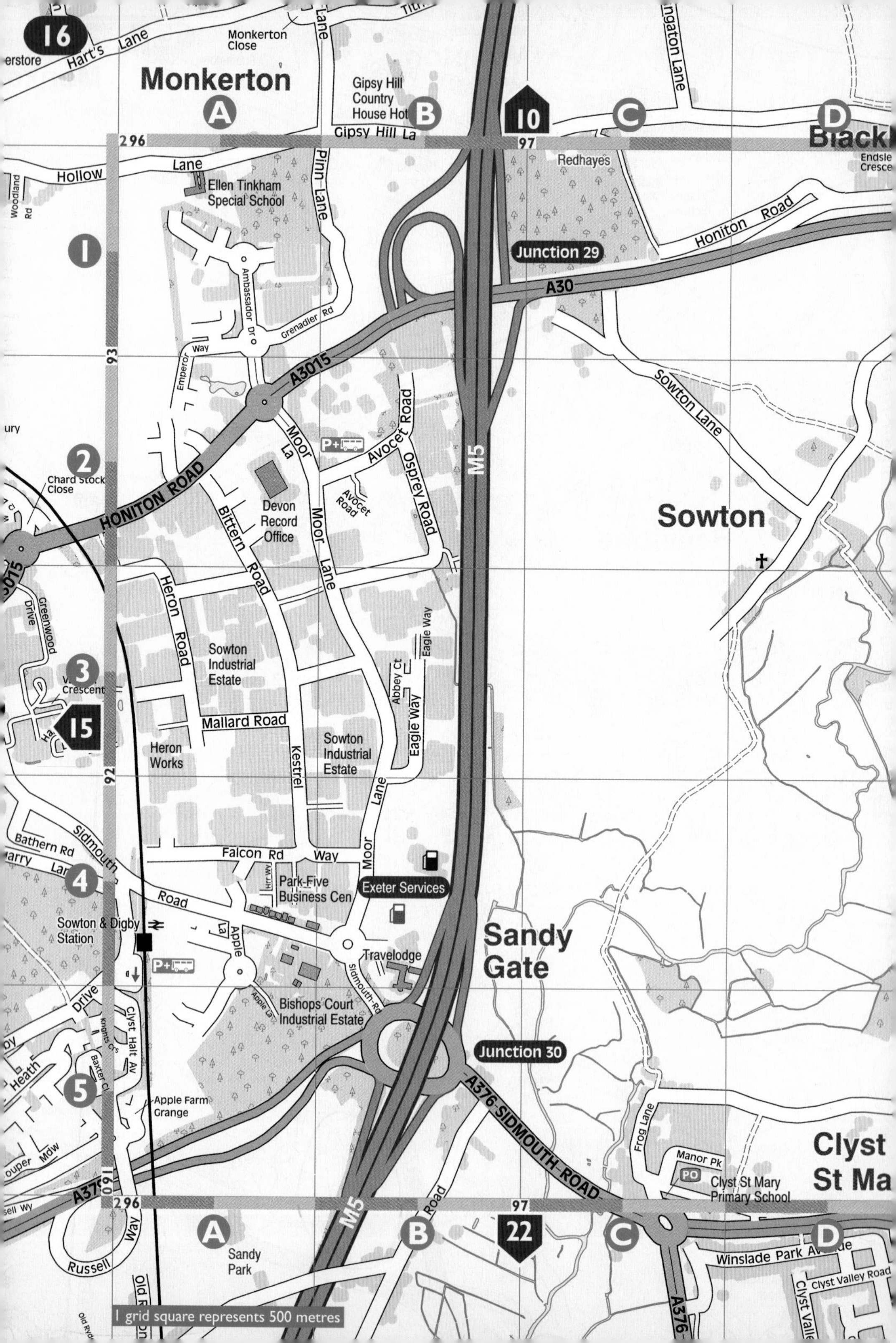
16
Hart's Lane
Monkerton Close
Monkerton
A
Gipsy Hill Country House Hot
B
Lane
Pinn Lane
Gipsy Hill La
10
C
D
296
97
Redhayes
Hollow
Lane
Woodland Rd
Ellen Tinkham Special School
Endsle Cresce
Honiton Road
1
Ambassador Dr
Grenadier Rd
Junction 29
A30
Emperor Way
93
A3015
Sowton Lane
Moor La
Avocet Road
2
Chard Stock Close
HONITON ROAD
Bittern Road
Devon Record Office
Moor Lane
Avocet Road
Osprey Road
M5
Sowton
Heron Road
Greenwood Drive
Sowton Industrial Estate
Eagle Way
Abbey Ct
3
Crescent
15
Mallard Road
Heron Works
Kestrel
Sowton Industrial Estate
Eagle Way
92
Lane
Sidmouth
Bathern Rd
Falcon Rd
Way
Moor
4
Park-Five Business Cen
Exeter Services
Road
Sowton & Digby Station
Apple La
Sandy Gate
Travelodge
Sidmouth Rd
Drive
Clyst Halt Av
Knights Crs
Apple La
Bishops Court Industrial Estate
Heath
Baxter Cl
Junction 30
5
Apple Farm Grange
A376 SIDMOUTH ROAD
Frog Lane
Manor Pk
PO
Clyst St Mary Primary School
Clyst St Ma
Mdw
91
296
97
Road
M5
A
B
22
C
D
Sandy Park
Winslade Park Avenue
Clyst Valley Road
Russell
Way
A376
1 grid square represents 500 metres

Waterslade Lane
Works
Ship La
St Michael's Cl
Clyst Honiton
Surgery
Honiton Road
Clyst Honiton School
Church Side
Exeter Airport
Exeter Industrial Estate
HONITON ROAD A30
B3184
A30
Dymond's Farm
Marlborough Farm
Bishop's Ct Lane
Wroford Manor
Holbrook Farm
Bishop's Court
Bishop's Court Lane
Westpoint (Devon County Showground)
Woodlands Way
Meadow Cl
Valley Rd
Glen Close
Axehayes Farm Caravan Site
Mushroom Rd
Blackmore Rd
Hill Barton Business Park
A3052
E
F
G
H
I
2
3
4
5
93
92
91
90
99
300
11
23

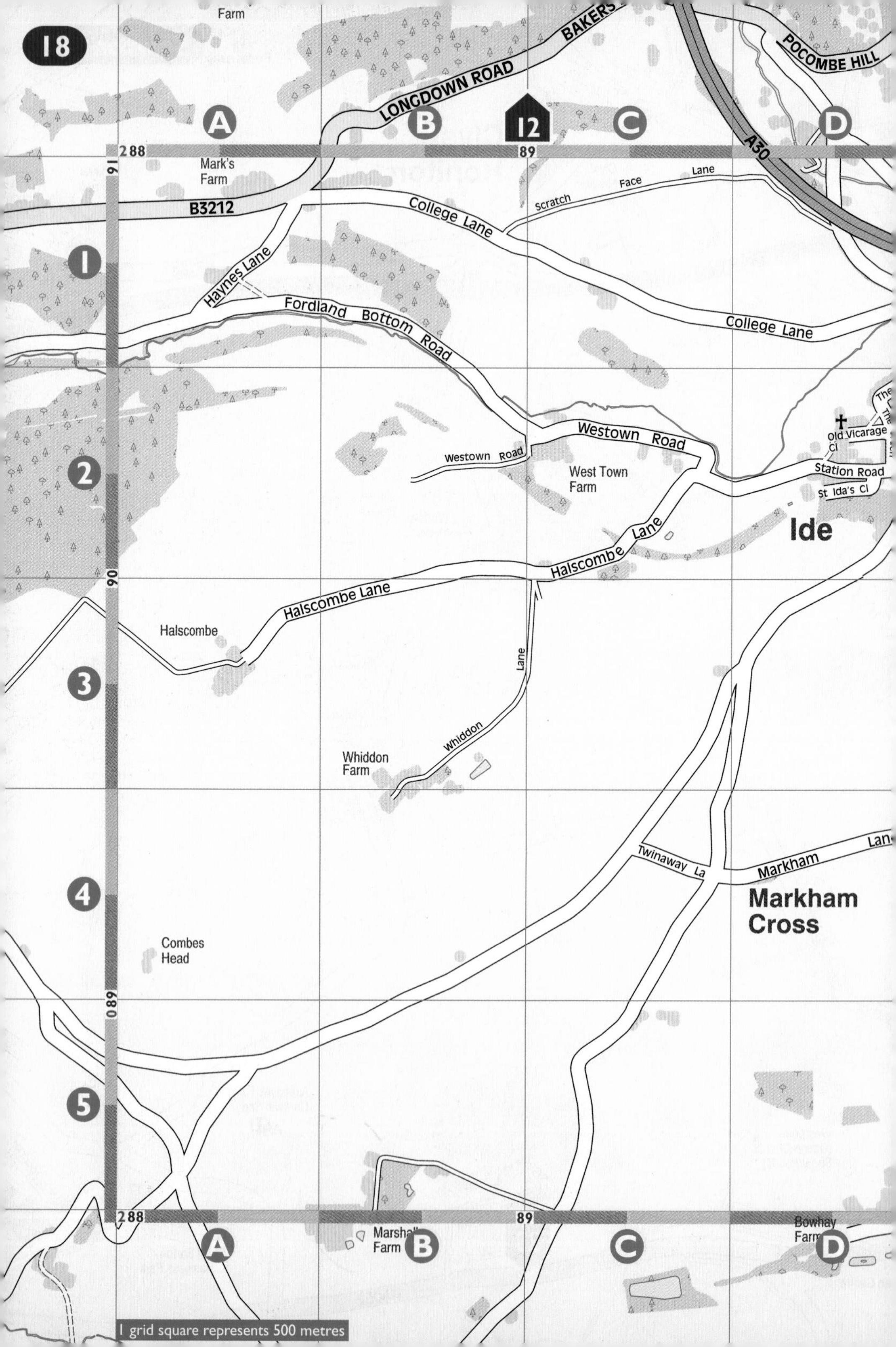
Farm
LONGDOWN ROAD
BAKERS
POCOMBE HILL
A
B
12
C
D
288
89
A30
Mark's Farm
91
B3212
College Lane
Scratch
Face
Lane
Haynes Lane
Fordland
Bottom
Road
College Lane
1
Westown Road
Westown Road
West Town Farm
The
Old Vicarage Cl
Station Road
St Ida's Cl
Ide
2
Halscombe Lane
Halscombe Lane
90
Halscombe
Lane
3
Whiddon
Whiddon Farm
Twinaway La
Markham
Lan
Markham Cross
4
Combes Head
089
5
288
89
A
B
C
D
Marshall Farm
Bowhay Farm
1 grid square represents 500 metres

St Thomas
Little John
Hambeer Lane
Vuefield Hl
Brdwy Hl
Orchard Hill
Franklyn Cl
Broadway
Parkway
Cowick Hill
Larch Rd
Cordery Rd
Pinces Rd
Queens
Waterloo Rd
Wellington Road
Poplar Cl
Taunton Cl
ALPHINGTON ROAD
Stone Lane Retail Park
Retail Pk
Marsh Barton Trading Est
Marsh Barton Rd
Percy Rd
Crtny Rd
Fortescue Rd
Woodville Rd
Ashton Rd
Ashton Business Cen
Trusham Rd
Bridford Rd
Christow Rd
Marsh Gn Rd
Marsh Gn Rd W
Marsh Gn Rd E
Newhayes Cl
Nwl Cl
Rexona Cl
Shelley Cl
Hatherleigh Road
Cowick Lane
Woodbury Vw
Saint Hl Cl
Balls Farm Road
West Exe Technology College
Superstore
Grace Road West
Grace Rd
Exeter St Thomas CC
Bradman Wy
Blenheim Road
Legion Way
Cross Vw
CHURCH ROAD B3123
PO
Alphington Sports Club
ALPHIN BROOK ROAD
B3123
Marsh Barton Trading Est
Old Ide La
A30
A377
Crabb Lane
Alphin Brook
Polehouse Lane
First School
Mandrake Rd
Mandrake Cl
Mill Lane
Brookfield Gardens
Powlesland Rd
Rosemont Ct
Chapel Rd
Budlake
Midway Close
Corn Mill Crs
Wheatsheaf Way
Alphington Combined School
Church Road
Clapperbrook La
Bate Cl
Ide Lane
Myrtle Cl
St Michael's Cl
Cem
Ide Lane
Ashleigh
Hwt Wy
Surg
D Cl
Bennett Cl
Aldens Rd
Cludens Cl
Lovelace Gdns
Dawlish Rd
Willsdown Rd
Alphing
Three C Place
Oakridge
Smith Field Road
Crtny Gdn
Fairfield Road
Arn Cl
Deacon Cl
Vestry Dr
Ragians
Mn Hll Cl
Loram Way
EX2
Colands Court
Ps Crt
Chantry Meadow
Ch Ct
Road
Hm C Wy
Wesley Wy
Steeple Dr
Lichgate Rd
Tower Walk
Pulpit Walk
Barnstone Ct
Veitch Gdns
Shillingford Rd
Royal Close
Markham Lane
Chudleigh Road
Markham Lane
Shillingford Road
Oak Cl
Waybrook Lane
Barrack Lane
Shillingford Abbot
Barton Lane
The Barton
91
92
90
89
E
F
G
H
I
2
3
4
5
12
13
20
24

20
14
19
25
A
B
C
D
1
2
3
4
5
292
93
91
90
89
Woodville Rd
Kennford
Exton Road
River Meadows
Water Lane
Rivermead Rd
Abbeville Cl
A3015
Buckerell Lodge Hotel
School
Shakespeare Road
Scott
Brooke Av
Spenser Av
Cowper Av
Dickens Dr
Tn Av
Chaucer Av
Milton Road
Lane
Knightley Rd
Salmonpool Lane
Ellard's Cl
Kg Henry's Rd
Old Abbey Ct
Briar Cres
Hamilton Av
TOPSHAM ROAD
University of Plymouth (Exeter Camous)
The Priory High School
Millbrook La
St Loyes Sch of Occupational Therapy
Exeter & Devon Crematorium
Retail/ Pk Cl
Marsh Barton Trading Est
Filmer Wy
Marsh Barton Rd
Marsh Gn Rd North
Trusham Rd
Bridford Rd
Christow Rd
Business Cen
Superstore
Marsh Gn Rd W
Marsh Gn Rd E
Dunns Business Centre
Exeter Canal
Grace Road West
Grace Road Central
Hennock Rd N
Exeter College
Exeter St Thomas CC
Bradman Wy
Cross Vw
PO
Alphington Sports Club
B3123
ALPHIN BROOK ROAD
Alphin Brook Road
Grace Rd S
Exe Valley Way
HENNOCK ROAD CENTRAL
Marsh Barton Trading Estate
River Exe
Powlesland Rd
Rosemont Ct
Church Road
Clapperbrook La
Budlake Road
Matford Pk Rd
Cofton Road
Cofton Rd
Hennock Road E
St Michael's
Lovelace Gdns
Dawlish Rd
Willsdown Rd
Trading Estate
Alphington
BAD HOMBURG WAY
Lustleigh Close
Denbury Ct
Silverton Road
Raglans
Three Corner Place
Manaton Cl
Matford Park Road
Deacon Cl
Chantry
Loram Way
Strawberry Avenue
Sigford Rd
Hm C Wy
Wesley Wy
Steeple
Lichgate Rd
Dawlish Road
Tower Walk
Kenbury Drive
Yeoford Way
Pulpit Walk
Chudleigh Road
A379
Devon Hotel
Old Matford La
Trood Lane
Wracombe Farm
Shep Hill
A30
Miller
1 grid square represents 500 metres

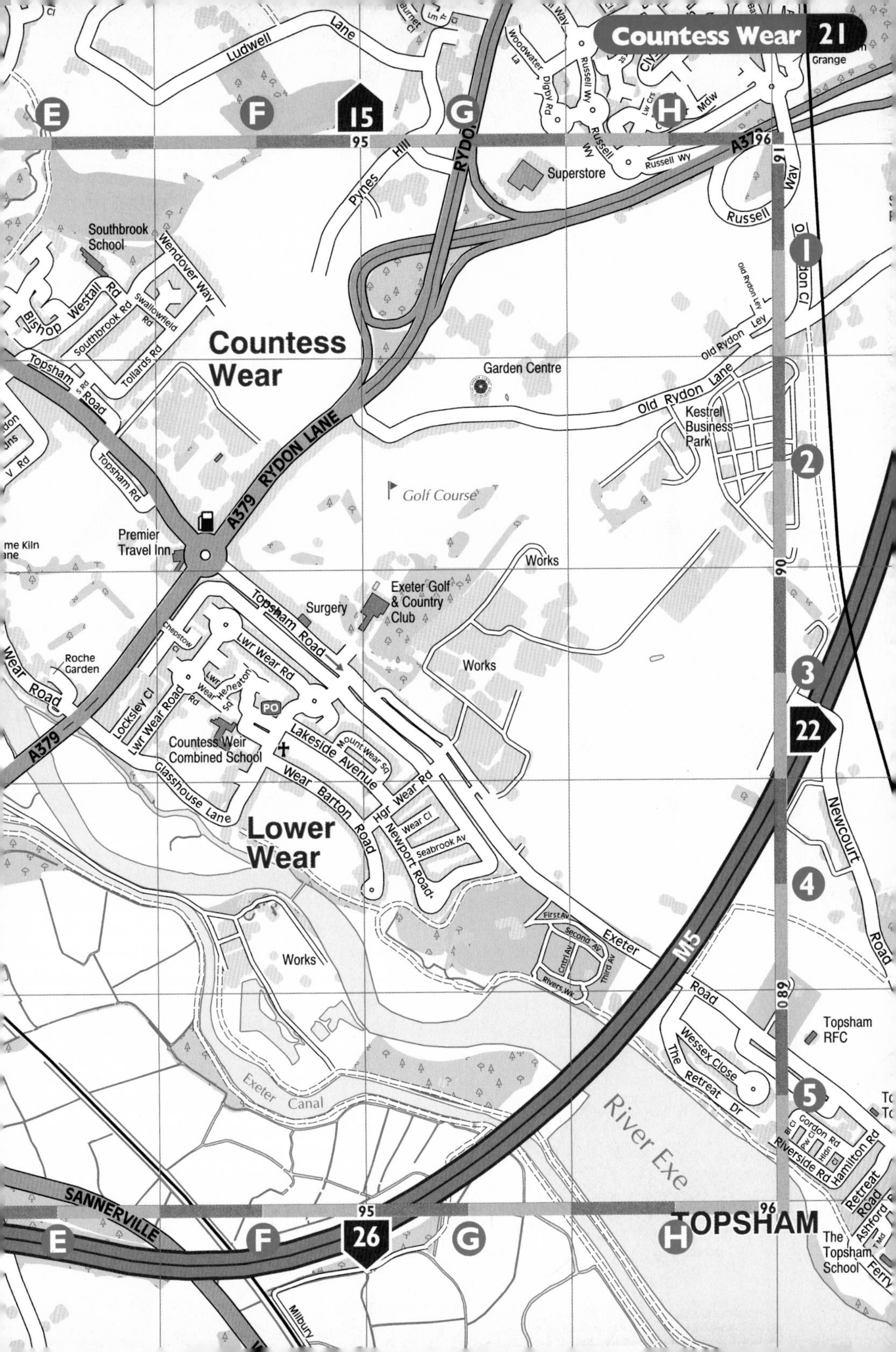

Countess Wear
Lower Wear
TOPSHAM
Ludwell Lane
Pynes Hill
Rydon Lane
A379 Rydon Lane
Superstore
Russell Way
Russell Wy
Digby Rd
Woodwater La
Southbrook School
Wendover Way
Bishop Westall Rd
Southbrook Rd
Swallowfield Rd
Tollards Rd
Topsham Road
Topsham Rd
Garden Centre
Old Rydon Lane
Old Rydon Ley
Kestrel Business Park
Golf Course
Premier Travel Inn
Works
Exeter Golf & Country Club
Surgery
Lwr Wear Rd
Chepstow Cl
Locksley Cl
Lwr Wear Road
Heneaton Sq
PO
Countess Weir Combined School
Lakeside Avenue
Mount Wear Sq
Wear Barton Road
Hgr Wear Rd
Newport Road
Wear Cl
Seabrook Av
Glasshouse Lane
Roche Garden
Wear Road
A379
First Av
Second Av
Third Av
Cntrl Av
Rivers Wk
Exeter Road
M5
Newcourt Road
Wessex Close
The Retreat Dr
Topsham RFC
Gordon Rd
Riverside Rd
Hamilton Rd
Retreat Road
Ashford Rd
Ferry Rd
The Topsham School
Exeter Canal
River Exe
Sannerville
Milbury
E
F
G
H
1
2
3
4
5
15
22
26
95
96

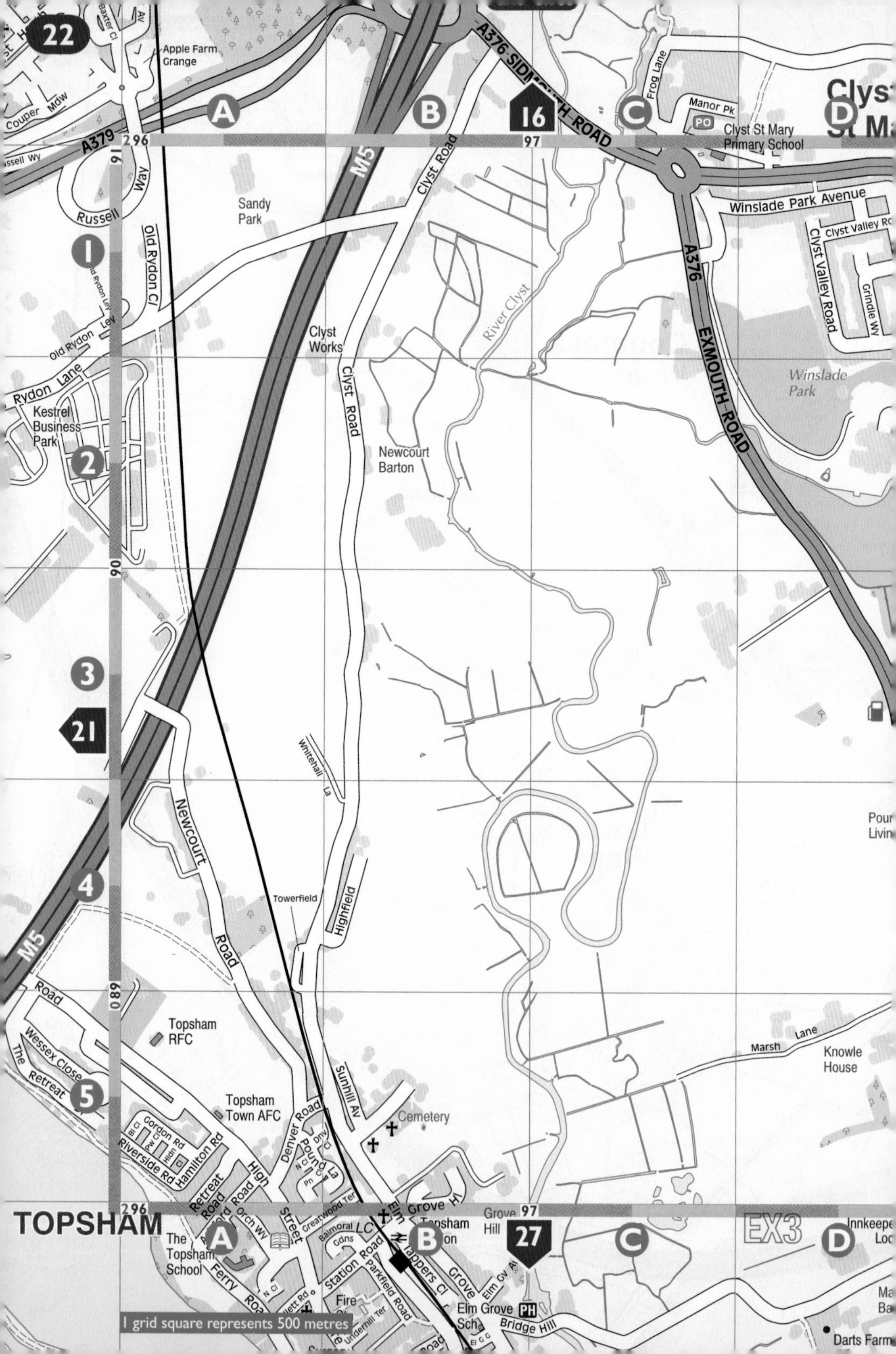
22
Apple Farm Grange
Couper Mdw
A379
Russell Way
Russell
Sandy Park
Old Rydon Cl
Old Rydon Ley
Old Rydon Lane
Rydon Lane
Kestrel Business Park
M5
Clyst Road
Clyst Works
A376 SIDMOUTH ROAD
16
Frog Lane
Manor Pk
PO
Clyst St Mary Primary School
Clyst St Mary
Winslade Park Avenue
Clyst Valley Rd
Clyst Valley Road
Grindle Wy
A376
EXMOUTH ROAD
River Clyst
Winslade Park
Newcourt Barton
21
Whitehall La
Newcourt Road
Towerfield
Highfield
Road
Wessex Close
The Retreat
Topsham RFC
Topsham Town AFC
Denver Road
Sunhill Av
Cemetery
Gordon Rd
Riverside Rd
Hamilton Rd
Retreat Road
High Street
Pound La
Greatwood Ter
Elm Grove Hl
Marsh Lane
Knowle House
TOPSHAM
The Topsham School
Ferry Road
Station Road
Parkfield Road
Balmoral Gdns
Happers Cl
Topsham Station
Grove Hill
27
Elm Grove Rd
Elm Grove
Elm Grove Sch
Bridge Hill
EX3
Innkeeper's Lodge
Darts Farm
1 grid square represents 500 metres
296
97
A
B
C
D
1
2
3
4
5

Westpoint (Devon County Showground)
E
F
17
G
H
99
300
Meadow Cl
Rosewood Crs
Close
Glen
H Rd
Blackmore
Blackmore Rd
Mushroom Rd
Mushroom Rd
Hill Barton Business Park
en Centre
A3052
I
Lane
C
B
Crealy Adventure Park
Greendale Lane
Oilmill Lane
Works
Grindle Brook
2
Shepherds Farm
Little Bridge Business Park
90
Courtbrook Farm
Kenniford Farm
3
Greendale Lane
Pytte Gardens
Pytte
Heathfield Farm
4
Lov
Higher
Clyst St George
89
Woodbury Rd
PO
Woodbury Rd
Clyst St George Lady Seawards CE Primary School
Bushayes Farm
5
B3179
Postlake Farm
99
300
E
F
28
G
H
WOODBURY ROAD
Ebford

Shillingford Abbot
Barrack Lane
Barton Lane
The Barton
19
A
B
C
D
290
91
1
2
3
4
5
88
87
86
Manstree
Manstree Road
The Willows
Ilex Cl
Shillingford St George
Sampson's Hill
New Barn Farm
Place Farm
Shillingford Lane
Peamore House
A379
pham
Brenton
Brenton Road
King's Road
Exeter Road
Pye Cnr
Rayners
PO
Sandfords
Kenn CE Primary School
Kennford
Stone Lane
Two
A38
The Firs
Bay Trees
Sandfords
Gissons La
30
Splatford Farm
Kennford International Caravan Park
1 grid square represents 500 metres

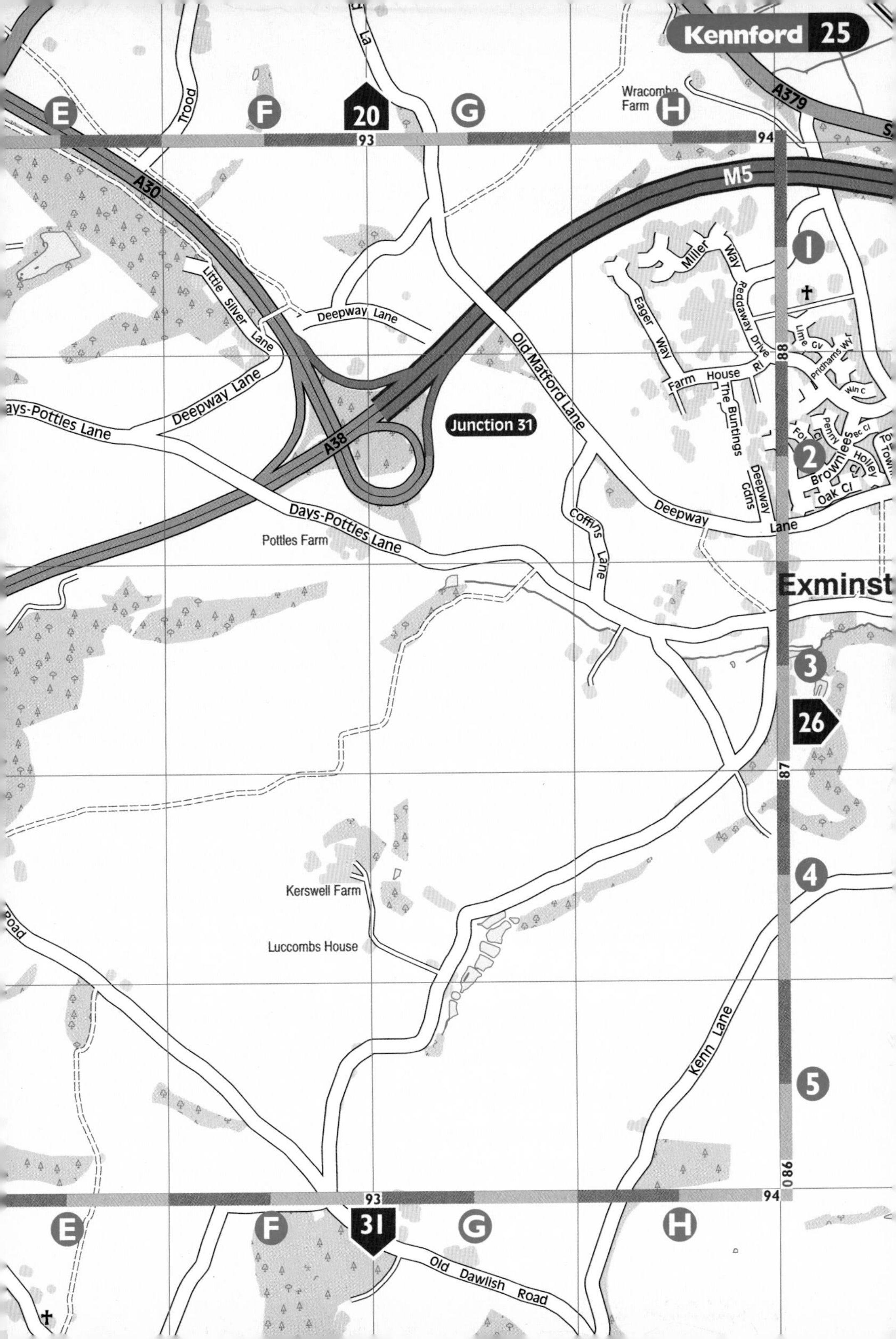
20
E
F
G
H
Trood
La
Wracombe Farm
A379
93
94
M5
A30
I
Miller Way
Eager Way
Reddaway Drive
Little Silver Lane
Deepway Lane
Old Matford Lane
Lime Gv
Pridhams Wy
Farm House Ri
88
Deepway Lane
Days-Pottles Lane
The Buntings
Win C
Junction 31
A38
Penny Cl
2
Brownlees
Holley Cl
Oak Cl
Deepway Gdns
Coffins Lane
Deepway Lane
Days-Pottles Lane
Pottles Farm
Exminst
3
26
87
4
Kerswell Farm
Road
Luccombs House
Kenn Lane
5
086
93
94
E
F
31
G
H
Old Dawlish Road

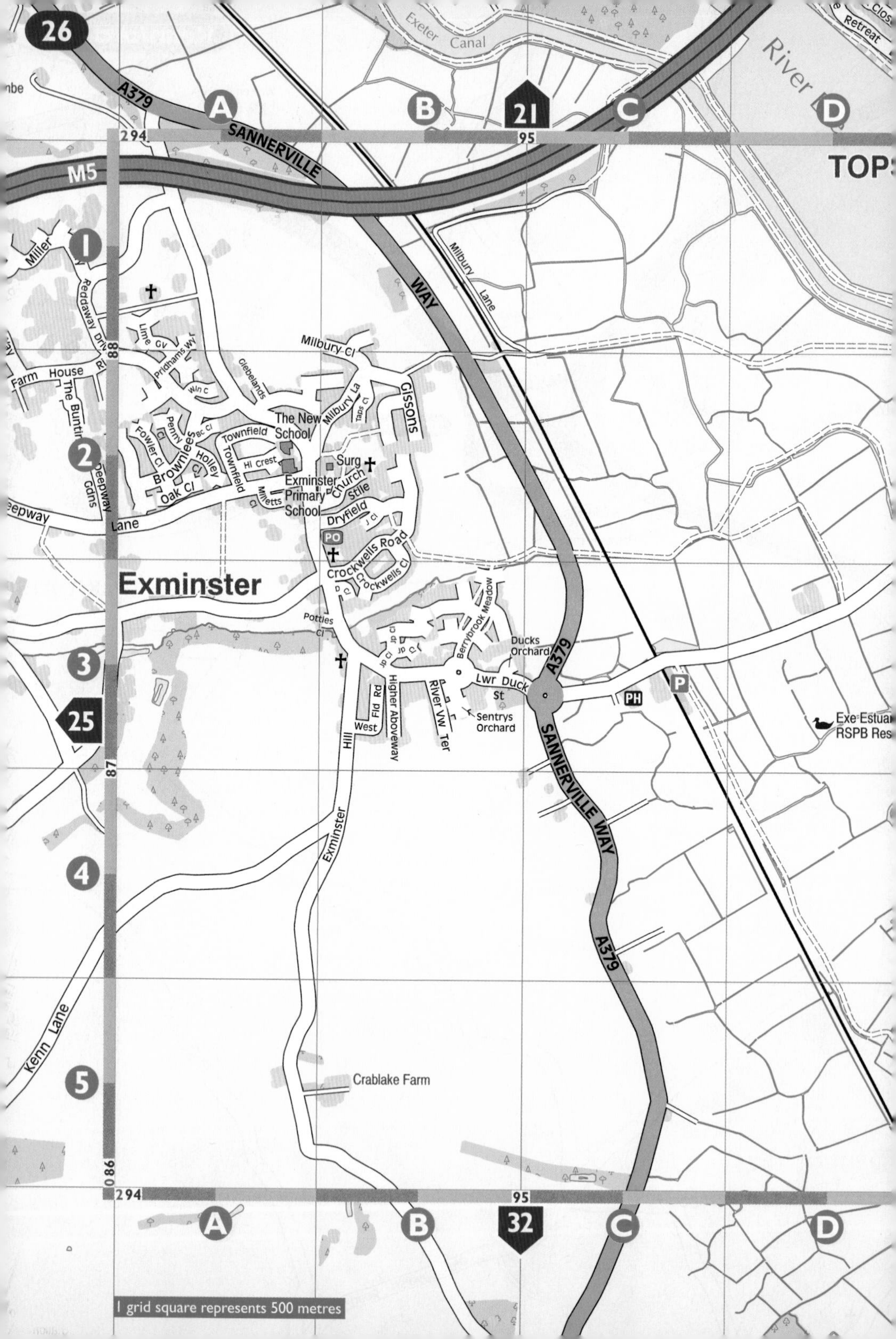
26
21
25
32
A
B
C
D
1
2
3
4
5
294
95
88
87
86
A379
SANNERVILLE WAY
M5
Exeter Canal
River
Retreat
TOPS
Miller
Reddaway Dr
Farm House Ri
The Buntings
Lime Gv
Pridhams Wy
Wln C
Clebelands
Milbury Lane
Milbury Cl
Milbury La
Taps Cl
Gissons
The New School
Surg
Penny Cl
Fowler Cl
Bc Cl
Brownlees
Holley Cl
Townfield
Hl Crest
Oak Cl
Deepway Gdns
Deepway Lane
Mlletts Cl
Exminster Primary School
Church Stile
Dryfield
J Cl
PO
Crockwells Road
Crockwells Cl
Exminster
Potties Cl
Berrybrook Meadow
Ducks Orchard
Lwr Duck St
Sentrys Orchard
River Vw Ter
Higher Aboveway
Fld Rd
West Hill
Exminster Hill
PH
P
Exe Estua
RSPB Res
Kenn Lane
Crablake Farm
1 grid square represents 500 metres

Topsham Town AFC
Cemetery
Sunhill Av
Denver Road
Pound La
Hamilton Rd
Retreat Road
High Street
Ashford Road
Orch Wy
Greatwood Ter
Elm Grove Hl
Topsham Station
Grove Hill
EX3
Innkeeper's Lodge
EXMOUTH RD
The Topsham School
Ferry Road
Balmoral Gdns
LC
Station Road
Tappers Cl
Grove Road
Elm Gv Av
Parkfield Road
Fire Stn
Underhill Ter
Follett Rd
Fore Street
Elm Grove
PH
Sch
Bridge Hill
Marsh Barton
Darts Farm
Ebf
Surgery
PO
Victoria Road
Globefield
Globe Lane
White St
Exe St
Topsham Sailing Club
Holman Way
Altamira
Monmouth St
Bowling Gn Road
Mh Av
Works
EXMOUTH ROAD
The Ridings
Old Ebford La
Monmouth Hl
Hope House Montessori School
Ntn St
Hgr Shapter St
Lower Shapter St
Topsham Museum
Strand Vw
Strand
Tresillian Gdns
Mount Howe
River Clyst
Riversmeet House
Station Road
South West Coast Path
A376
28
EXMOUTH
Exeter Canal
Green Lane
River Front
Exton
Sandpiper Drive
Exton Lane
Nurseries Close
Exton Station
Station Rd
Turf
22
33
97
98
88
87
86
E
F
G
H
1
2
3
4
5
Lympstone Commando Station
House

28
ouse
Clyst St George
Lady Seawards
CE Primary School
Woodbury Rd
Bushayes Farm
Chapel Hill
B3179
EXMOUTH RD
A
B
23
C
D
Postlake Farm
298
99
Innkeeper's Lodge
Marsh Ba
1
Darts Farm
Ebford
A376
WOODBURY ROAD
Ebford Lane
88
EXMOUTH ROAD
The Ridings
Lower Lane
B3179
2
Old Ebford La
Higher Bagmores Farm
3
A376
Lower Bagmores Farm
27
Rydon Far
87
EXMOUTH ROAD
Green Lane
4
River
Mill Lane
Rydon Lane
Exton
PH
Sandpiper Drive
Exton Lane
Barton Cl
Front
Exton Station
Nurseries Close
Btn Ms
Station Road
Station Rd
5
The Avenue
Lane
86
298
99
A
B
34
Porter's
C
D
Stony Lan
Lympstone
Station
1 grid square represents 500 metres
A376

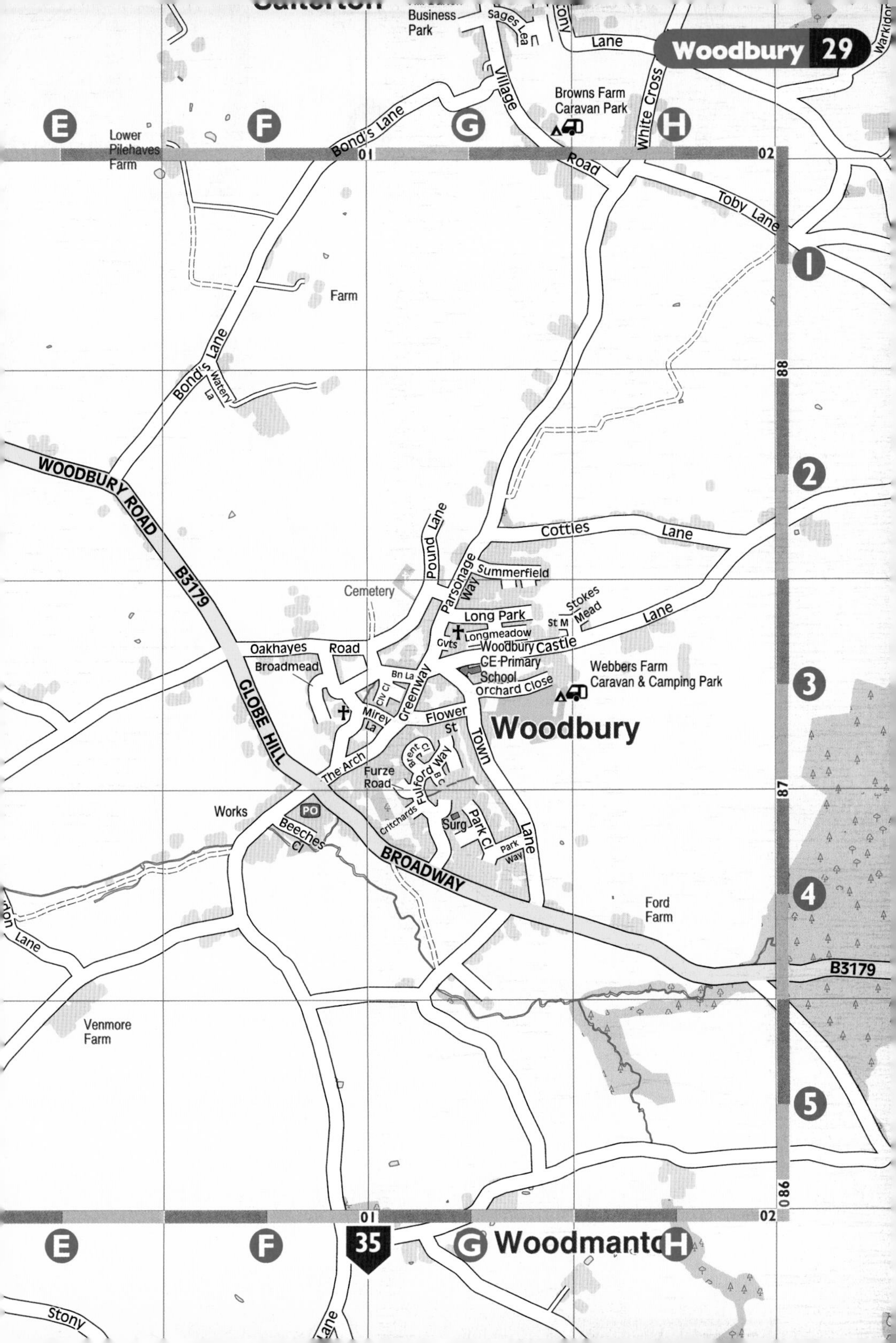
Business Park
Sages Lea
Lane
Village
Browns Farm Caravan Park
White Cross
Road
Bond's Lane
Lower Pilehaves Farm
E
F
G
H
01
02
Toby Lane
1
Farm
Bond's Lane
Watery La
88
WOODBURY ROAD
B3179
2
Pound Lane
Cottles
Lane
Parsonage Way
Summerfield
Cemetery
Long Park
Stokes Mead
St M
Lane
Longmeadow
Gvts
Woodbury Castle
Oakhayes
Road
Broadmead
Bn La
Cliv Cl
Greenway
GE Primary School
Orchard Close
Webbers Farm Caravan & Camping Park
3
Mirey La
Flower St
Town
Woodbury
GLOBE HILL
Brent Cl
Fulford Way
The Arch
Furze Road
87
Works
PO
Critchards
Surg
Park Cl
Park Way
Lane
Beeches Cl
BROADWAY
4
Ford Farm
Lane
B3179
Venmore Farm
5
086
35
Woodmanton
Stony
Lane

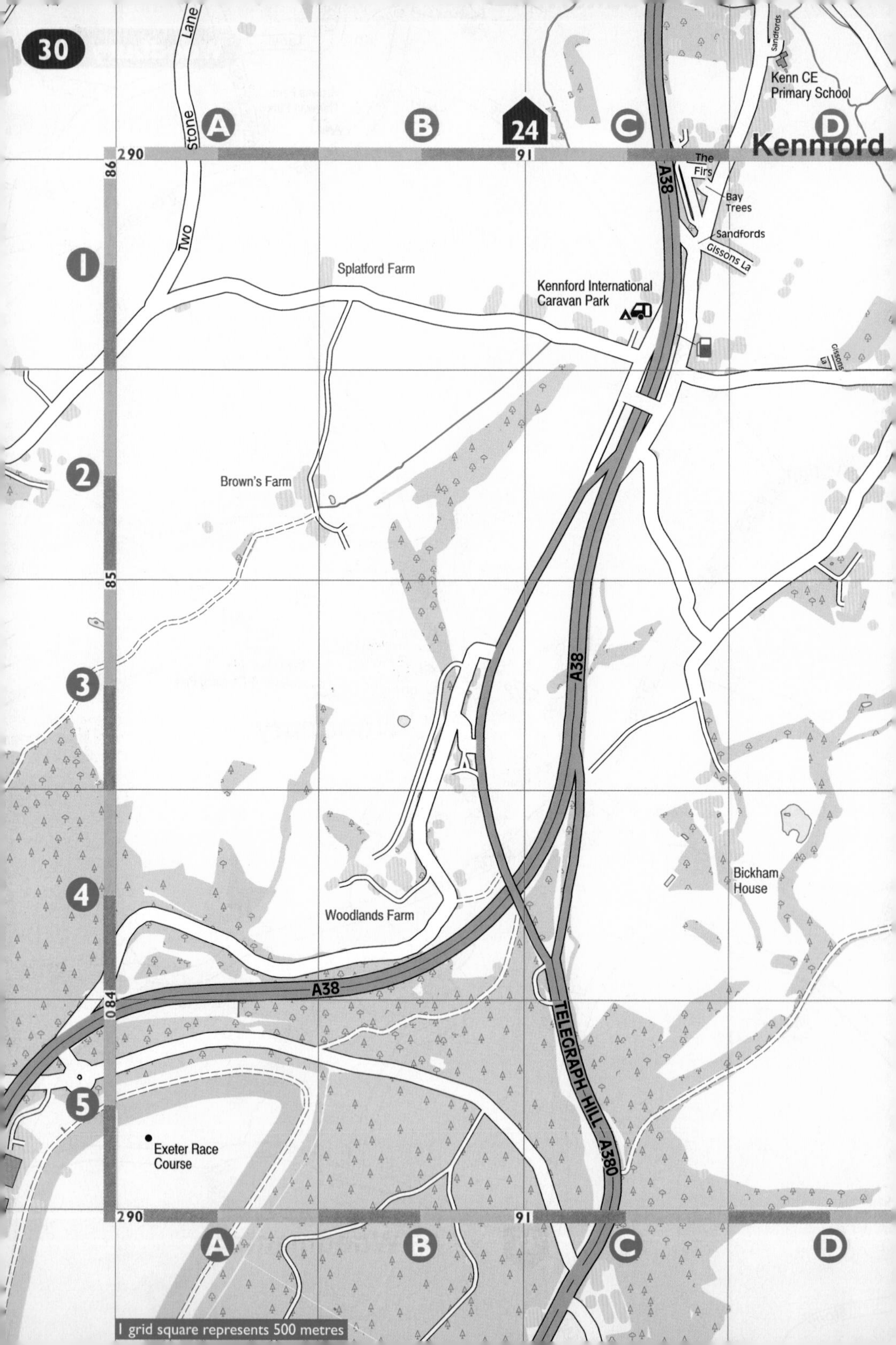
24
Kenford
Kenn CE
Primary School
Sandfords
The
Firs
Bay
Trees
Sandfords
Gissons La
Gissons
La
Two
Stone
Lane
Splatford Farm
Kennford International
Caravan Park
Brown's Farm
A38
A38
A38
Woodlands Farm
Bickham
House
TELEGRAPH HILL
A380
Exeter Race
Course
A
B
C
D
1
2
3
4
5
290
91
86
85
84
1 grid square represents 500 metres

25
E
F
G
H
93
94
86
Kenn
Old Dawlish Road
Works
River Kenn
Old Dawlish Road
1
2
85
Pennycombe Farm
3
32
vorthy Far
4
Whitcombe
084
5
Haydon Common
n Farm
93
94
E
F
G
H

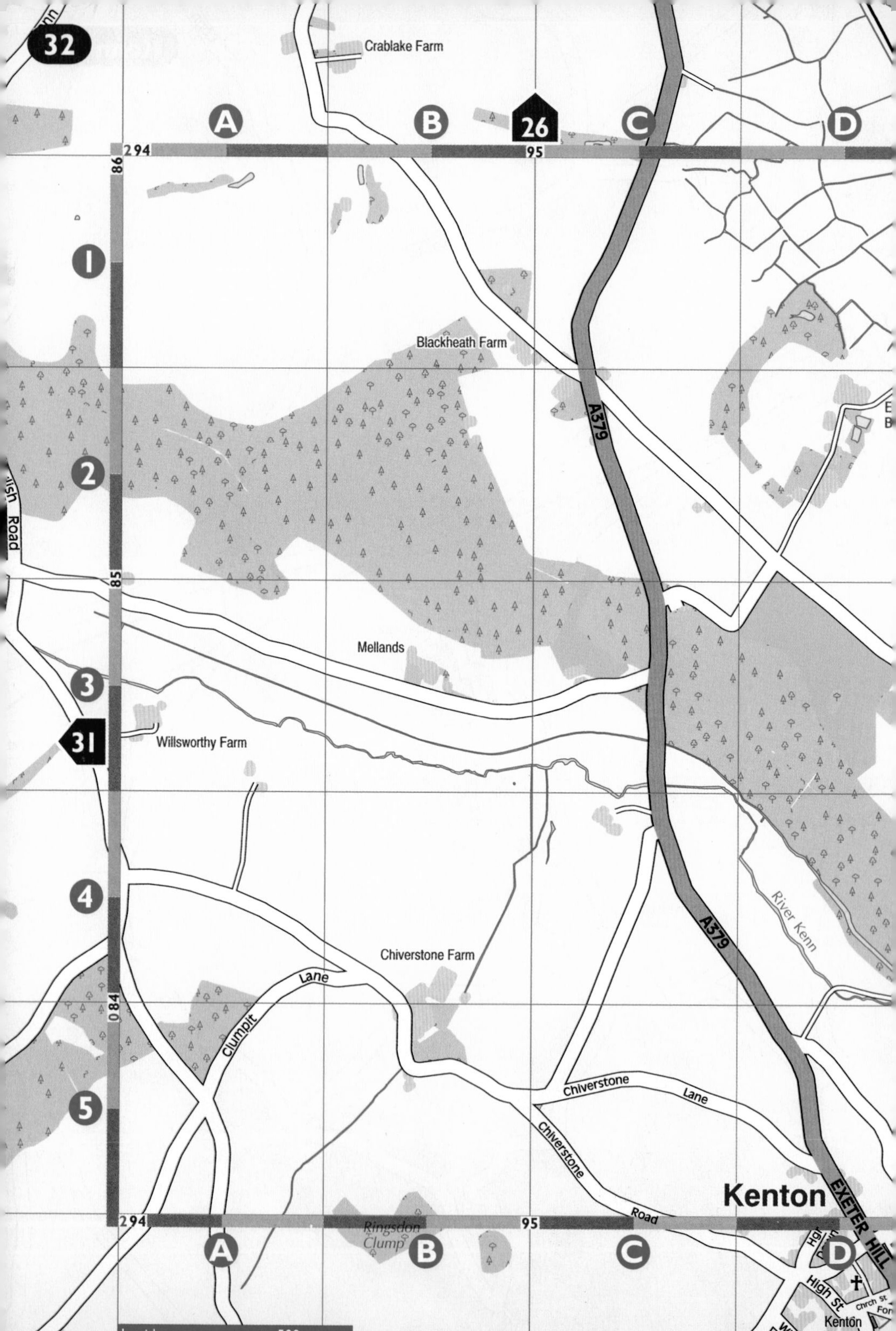

1 grid square represents 500 metres

Station Rd
Turf
PH
E
F
27
G
H
97
98
86
1
Lympstone Commando Station
South West Coast Path
River Exe
2
85
3
34
Powderham
Church Road
4
Starcross Yacht Club
084
5
Powderham Castle
97
98
E
F
36
G
H
Penhayes Rd

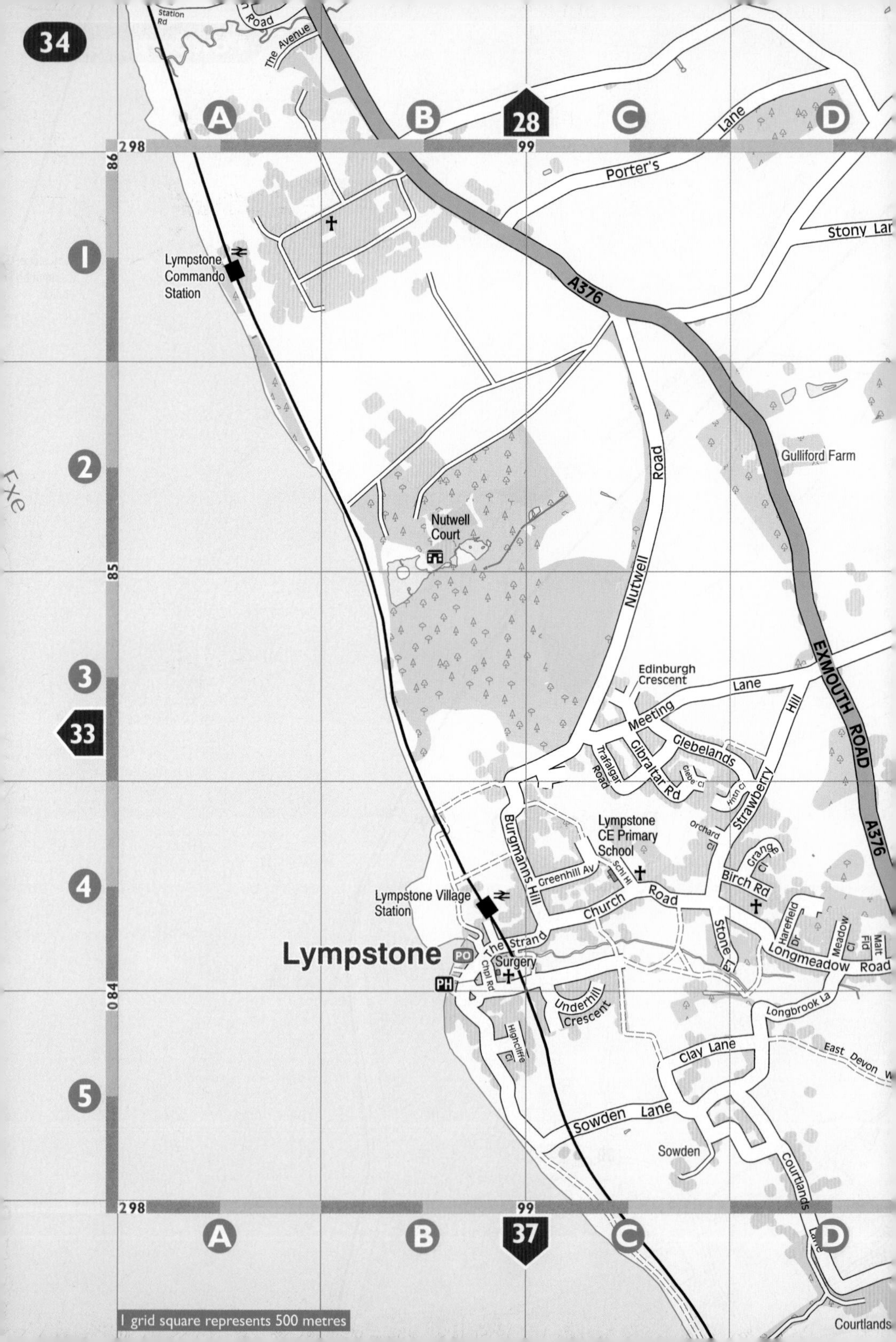
Station Rd
Road
The Avenue
A
B
28
C
D
298
99
86
Porter's
Lane
Stony Lar
1
Lympstone Commando Station
A376
2
Exe
Road
Gulliford Farm
Nutwell Court
85
Nutwell
3
33
EXMOUTH ROAD
Edinburgh Crescent
Meeting
Lane
Hill
Trafalgar Road
Gibraltar Rd
Glebelands
Glebe Cl
Strawberry
Orchard Cl
Lympstone CE Primary School
Burgmanns Hill
Greenhill Av
Schl Hl
4
Lympstone Village Station
Church
Road
Birch Rd
Grange Cl
Stone La
Harefield Dr
Meadow Cl
Malt Fld
A376
Lympstone
PO
The Strand
Surgery
Longmeadow Road
Chpl Rd
PH
084
Underhill Crescent
Longbrook La
Highcliffe Cl
Clay Lane
East Devon W
5
Sowden Lane
Sowden
Courtlands Lane
298
99
A
B
37
C
D
1 grid square represents 500 metres
Courtlands

E
F
29
G
H
01
02
86
Woodmanton
I
Stony
Lane
Tedstone Lane
2
Coombe
Farm
Road
Harefield
85
Exe View Road
Tedstone
House
Watton Brook
3
Peters
hool
Harefield
Tedstone Lane
Marley
Drive
4
Marley
Hayes
Wotton
Lane
Road
084
Rd
Hulham
Marley
Dorchester
Way
Shirley
Close
Winchester Dr
5
Dinan Way
Keats
Cl
Shakespeare Way
Clr Cl
Tennyson Wy
Whitman Cl
Thomas Cl
Milton
Wrdswrth
Marley
Road
Bunn
Road
Gorse La
Bystock Road
Diane
Lincoln
Cl
Canterbury Way
Truro Drive
Nrw Cl
O Cl
Herefrd Cl
Brittany Rd
Pitt Farm
ROAD
Summer
Lane
01
02
Bystoc
38
E
F
G
H
A La Ronde
NT
East Devon Way
Drive
Hill
Littlemead
A376
Swiss Cl
April Cl
Pleasant
Thorpe
Av
Ap Cl
O Cl
Hulham Road
Betjemen
Dr
Way
Lvng
Comilla
Close
Barrowdale
Close
Rowlstone
Close
Hollymount Cl
Drive
Surgery
Mrc Cl
Palm
Cl
Redwood
Maple Dr
Holly
Wk
Evergreen Cl
Valley
Sherwood
Dr
Dinan
Pine
Cedar
Lane
Rd
Cester Rd

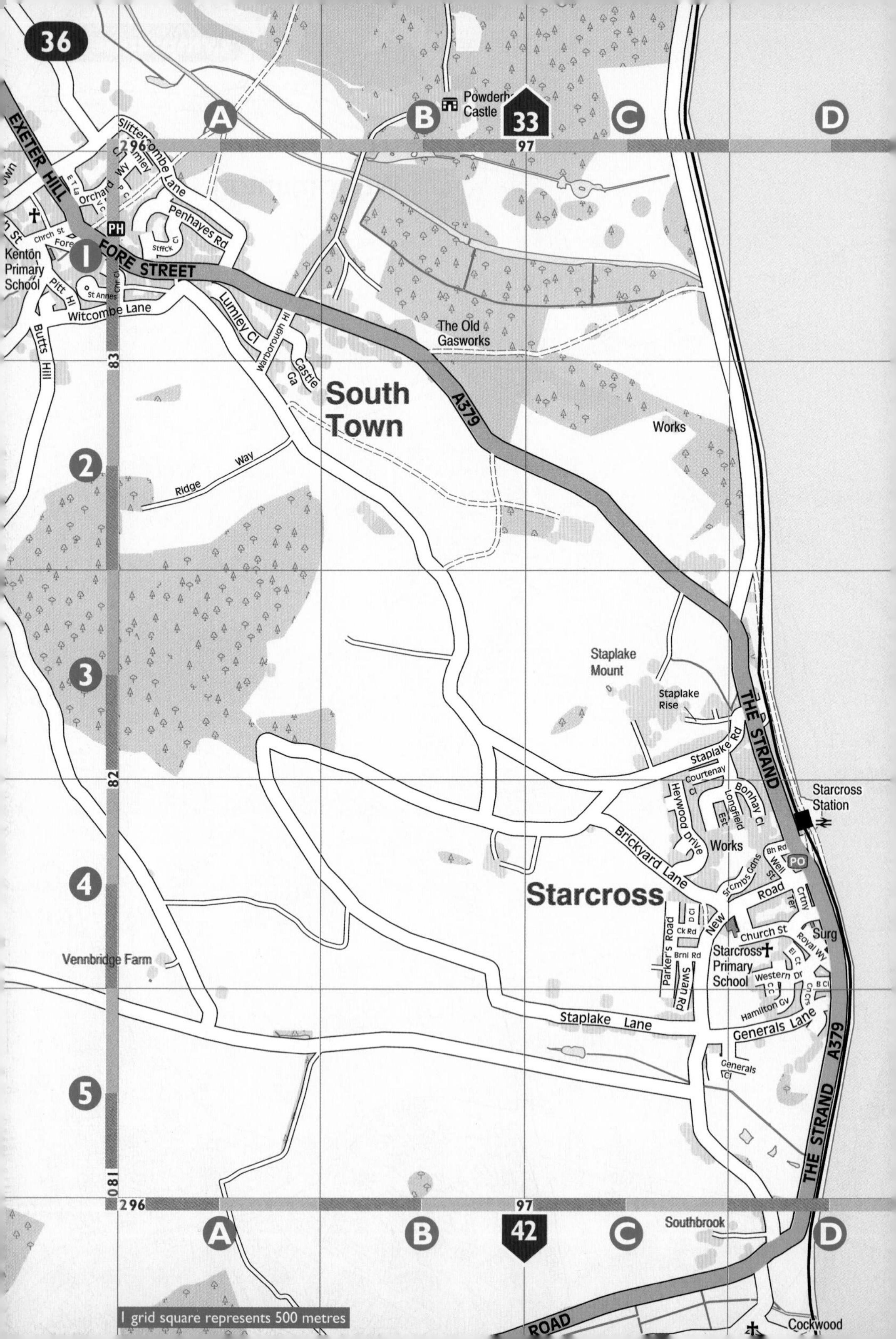
A
B
C
D
33
97
296
Powderham Castle
EXETER HILL
FORE STREET
Slittercombe Lane
Orchard Wy
Penhayes Rd
Stffck Cl
Chrch St
Fore St
Kenton Primary School
Pitt Hl
St Annes
Witcombe Lane
Butts Hill
Lumley Cl
Warborough Hl
Castle Ga
The Old Gasworks
South Town
A379
Works
Ridge Way
83
82
81
80
1
2
3
4
5
Staplake Mount
Staplake Rise
THE STRAND
Staplake Rd
Courtenay Cl
Bonhay Cl
Heywood Drive
Longfield Est
Starcross Station
Brickyard Lane
Works
Bh Rd
Well St
PO
Stcmbs Gdns
Starcross
New Road
Ter
Crtny
D Cl
Ck Rd
Church St
Surg
Royal Wy
Starcross Primary School
Parker's Road
Brnl Rd
Swan Rd
El Ct
Western Dr
B Cl
Cn Crs
Hamilton Gv
Vennbridge Farm
Staplake Lane
Generals Lane
Generals Cl
THE STRAND A379
42
Southbrook
ROAD
Cockwood
1 grid square represents 500 metres

Sowden Lane
Sowden
Courtlands Lane
Courtlands
34
E
F
G
H
I
99
300
83
2
3
4
5
Seafield Avenue
Featherbed
Crossingfields Drive
Highbury Park
Carberry Avenue
38
Halsdon Av
82
Carter Av
Southern Rd
FC
A376 MARINE WAY
Woodville Rd
Hartopp Road
Halsdon Rd
Salisbury Road
Rosebery Road
Egrmnt Road
Church Rd
River Exe
The Royal Av
MARINE WAY
Bus Stn
New Nth Rd
New St
Exmouth Station
Exmouth Indoor Market
Parade
The Point
Exmouth RFC
81
Estuary Road
Exe Sailing
43
Surgery
Camperdown Ter
Point Ter
Shelly Road
Victoria Way
Victoria Road
Wrks
Imperial
Morton
Exmouth Leisure Cen
Primary Sch
ROLLE STREET
Queen St
Market
Church
Manor
PO

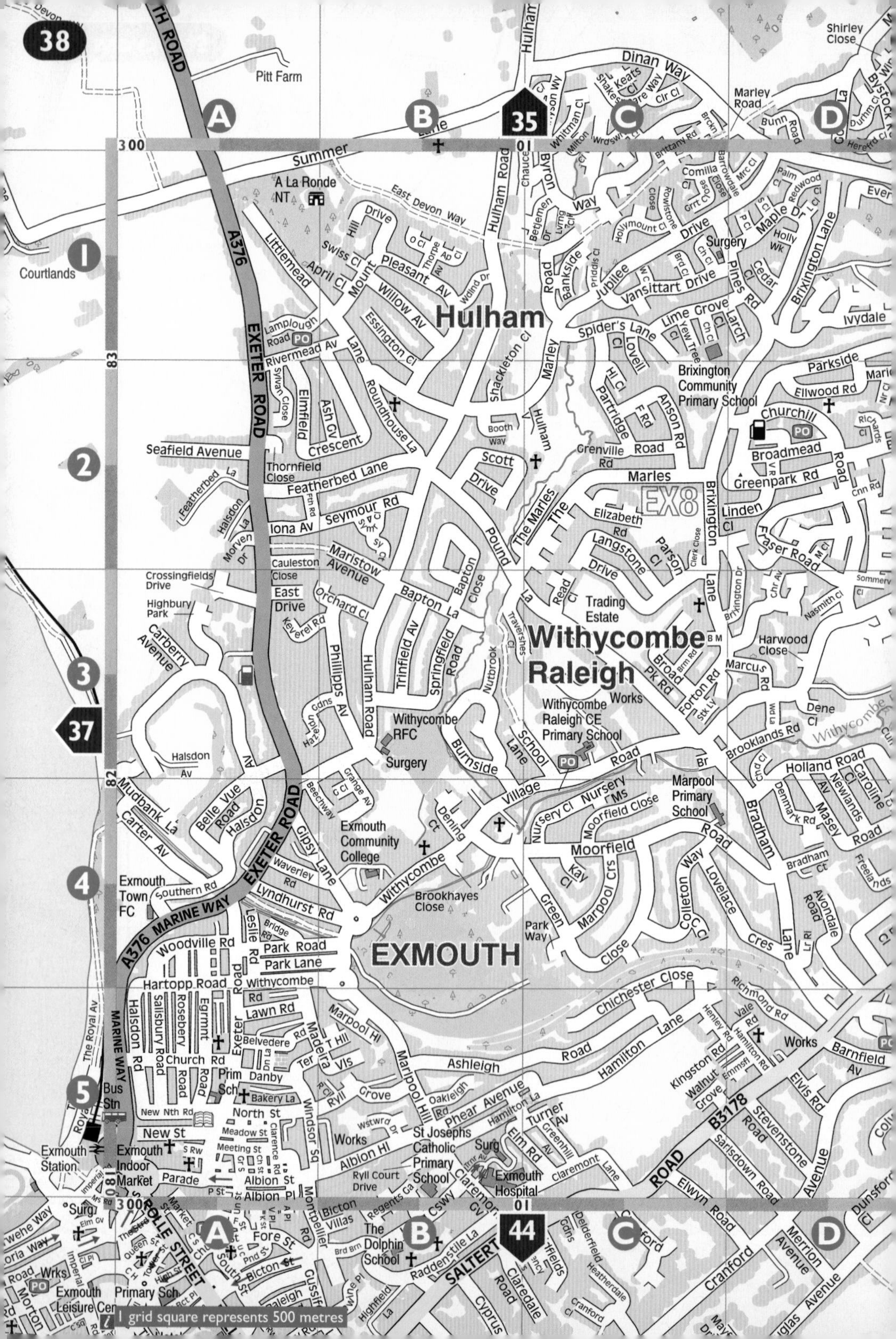
Pitt Farm
Summer Lane
A La Ronde NT
East Devon Way
Courtlands
A376
EXETER ROAD
Hulham
Hulham Road
Dinan Way
Keats Cl
Shakespeare Way
Whitman Cl
Byron Way
Chaucer
Milton
Betjemen Dr
Bankside
Jubilee Drive
Vansittart Drive
Surgery
Pines Rd
Maple Dr
Holly Wk
Brixington Lane
Marley Road
Bunn Road
Bystock
Shirley Close
Ivydale
Littlemead
April Cl
Swiss Cl
Mount Pleasant Av
Hill Drive
Thorpe Av
Willow Av
Essington Cl
Lamplough Road
Rivermead Av
Sylvan Close
Elmfield Crescent
Ash Gv
Roundhouse La
Shackleton Cl
Marley
Spider's Lane
Lime Grove
Yew Tree
Lovell Cl
Larch Cl
Brixington Community Primary School
Parkside
Ellwood Rd
Churchill
Richards
Broadmead
Greenpark Rd
Linden Cl
Fraser Road
Partridge Road
Anson Rd
Grenville Rd
Marles
The Marles
The
Elizabeth Rd
Langstone Drive
Parson Cl
Clerk Close
Brixington Dr
EX8
Seafield Avenue
Thornfield Close
Featherbed Lane
Featherbed La
Halsdon La
Iona Av
Seymour Rd
Morven Dr
Booth Way
Scott Drive
Pound
Bapton Close
Bapton La
Maristow Avenue
Caulestone Close
East Drive
Crossingfields Drive
Highbury Park
Carberry Avenue
Orchard Cl
Keverel Rd
Phillipps Av
Hulham Road
Trinfield Av
Springfield Road
Nutbrook
Travershes Cl
Read Cl
Trading Estate
Withycombe Raleigh
Works
Broad Pk Rd
Forton Rd
Harwood Close
Marcus Rd
Nasmith Cl
Dene Cl
Brooklands Rd
Withycombe
Hazeldon Gdns
Withycombe RFC
Surgery
Burnside
School Lane
Withycombe Raleigh CE Primary School
Village Road
Halsdon Av
Mudbank La
Belle Vue Road
Halsdon
Carter Av
Grange Av
Beechway
Exmouth Community College
Dening Ct
Nursery Cl
Nursery Ms
Moorfield Close
Marpool Primary School
Bradham
Holland Road
Caroline
Newlands Cl
Masey Road
Denmark Rd
Bradham Ct
Avondale Road
Freelands
Exmouth Town FC
Southern Rd
Waverley Rd
Gipsy Lane
Lyndhurst Rd
Withycombe
Brookhayes Close
Moorfield
Kay Cl
Marpool Crs
Green
Park Way
Close
Colleton Way
Lovelace Cres
Bradham Lane
A376 MARINE WAY
Woodville Rd
Leslie Rd
Park Road
Park Lane
EXMOUTH
Hartopp Road
Withycombe Rd
Chichester Close
Richmond Rd
Halsdon Rd
Salisbury Road
Rosebery Road
Egrmnt
Exeter Road
Lawn Rd
Belvedere Rd
Marpool Hl
Madeira Vls
Ashleigh Road
Hamilton Lane
Henley Rd
Vale Rd
Hamilton Rd
Works
Barnfield Av
Elvis Rd
Church Rd
Danby Ter
Prim Sch
Bakery La
Grove
Marpool Hill
Oakleigh Rd
Phear Avenue
Hamilton La
Kingston Rd
Walnut Grove
B3178
Stevenstone Road
Bus Stn
New Nth Rd
North St
Meadow St
New St
Meeting St
Windsor Sq
Works
Albion Hl
St Josephs Catholic Primary School
Surg
Elm Rd
Turner Av
Greenhill Av
Claremont Lane
ROAD
Sarlsdown Road
Avenue
Exmouth Station
Exmouth Indoor Market
Parade
Albion St
Albion Pl
Ryll Court Drive
Exmouth Hospital
Elwyn Road
Dunsford Cl
MARINE WAY
The Royal Av
Royal
Imperial
Surg.
ROLLE STREET
Fore St
Bicton St
Bicton Villas
Montpellier Rd
Regents Ga
The Dolphin School
Raddenstile La
SALTERTON
Claredale Road
Cranford
Merrion Avenue
Douglas Avenue
Exmouth Leisure Cen
Primary Sch
Morton
Wrks
Cyprus
Highfield
Heatherdale
1 grid square represents 500 metres

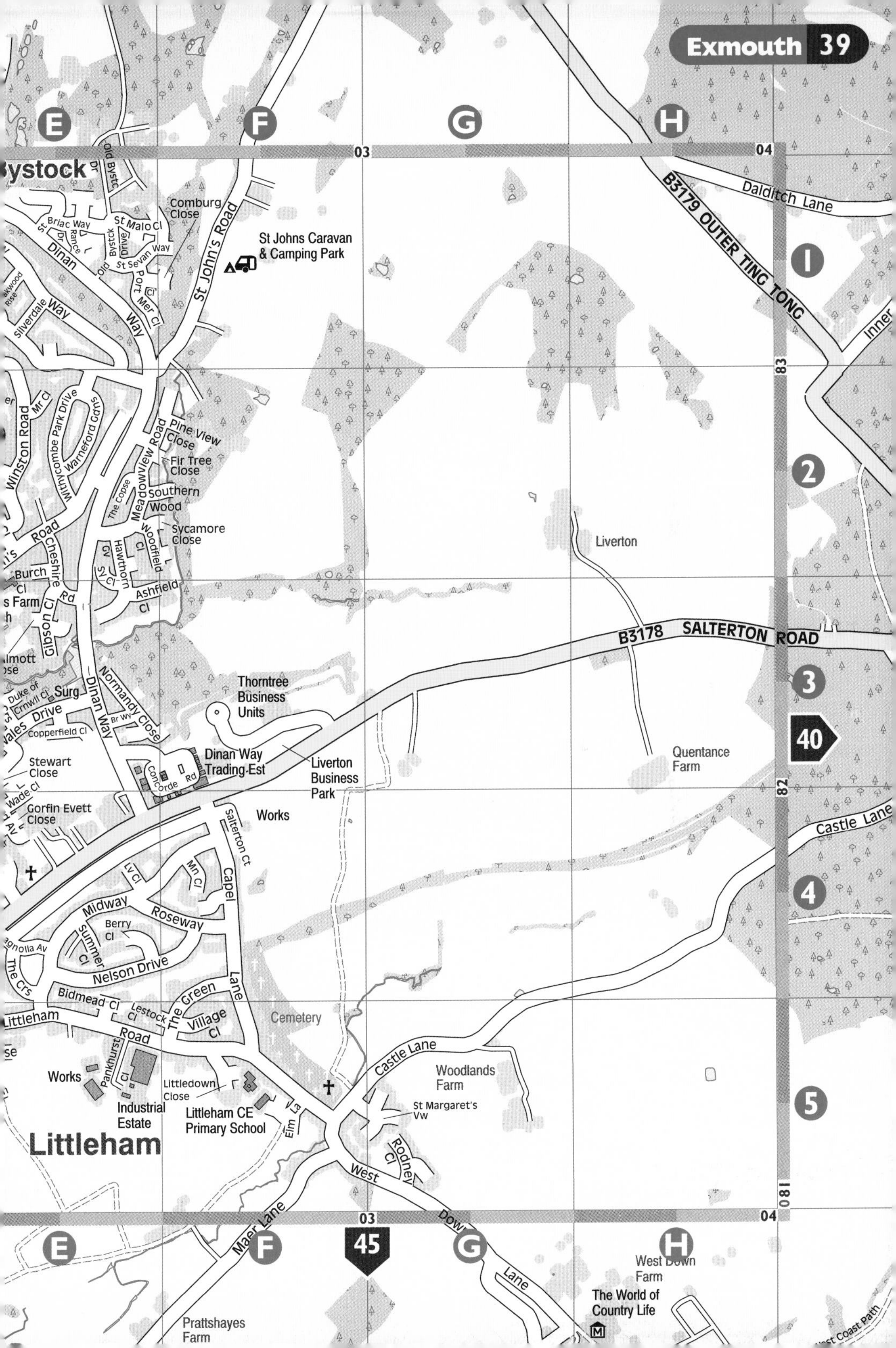
E
F
G
H
03
04
Bystock
Old Bystc Dr
Comburg Close
St Johns Caravan & Camping Park
St John's Road
St Briac Way
Dr Rance
St Malo Cl
Old Bystck Drive
St Sevan Way
Port Mer Cl
Cl
Dinan Way
Silverdale Way
Oakwood Rise
Dalditch Lane
B3179 OUTER TING TONG
Inner
1
2
3
4
5
83
82
81
80
Winston Road
Mr Cl
Withycombe Park Drive
Warneford Gdns
Meadowview Road
Pine View Close
Fir Tree Close
The Copse
Southern Wood
Sycamore Close
Woodfield Cl
Hawthorn Gv
St Cl
Ashfield Cl
Cheshire Rd
Burch Cl
s Farm
Gibson Cl
Road
Liverton
B3178 SALTERTON ROAD
Thorntree Business Units
Normandy Close
Dinan Way
Br Wy
Duke of Crnwll Cl
Surg
Wales Drive
Copperfield Cl
Stewart Close
Wade Cl
Gorfin Evett Close
Av
Dinan Way Trading Est
Concorde Rd
Liverton Business Park
Quentance Farm
40
Castle Lane
Works
Salterton Ct
Capel Lane
Lv Cl
Mn Cl
Midway
Roseway
Berry Cl
Summer Cl
Magnolia Av
The Crs
Nelson Drive
Bidmead Cl
Lestock Cl
The Green
Village Cl
Littleham Road
Cemetery
Castle Lane
Woodlands Farm
Works
Pankhurst Cl
Littledown Close
Industrial Estate
Littleham CE Primary School
Elm La
St Margaret's Vw
Rodney Cl
Littleham
West Down Lane
Maer Lane
45
West Down Farm
The World of Country Life
Prattshayes Farm
East Coast Path

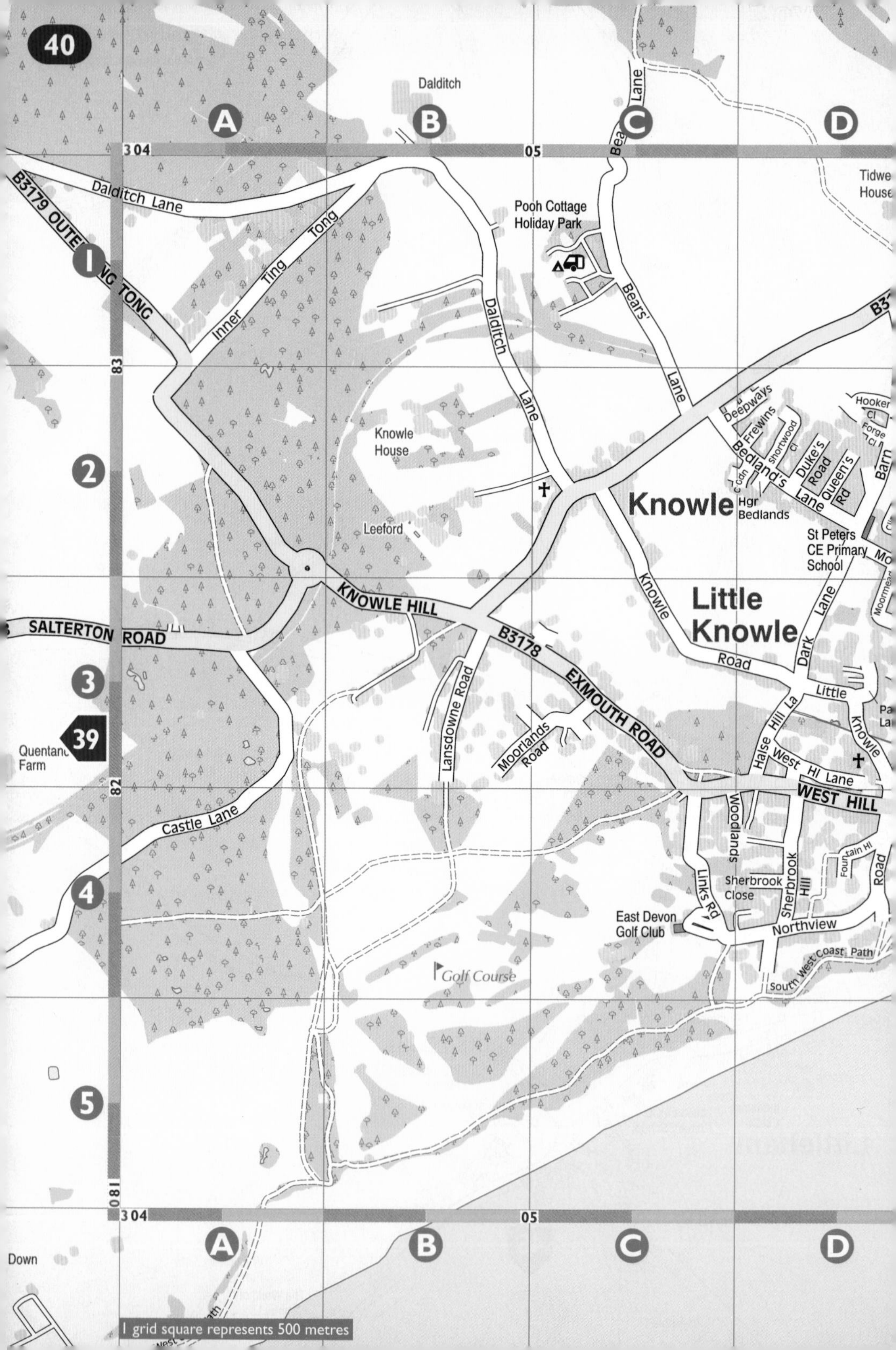
Dalditch
A
B
C
D
304
05
Bears' Lane
Tidwell House
Dalditch Lane
B3179 OUTER TING TONG
Inner Ting Tong
Pooh Cottage
Holiday Park
Bears' Lane
Dalditch Lane
83
1
2
3
4
5
Knowle House
Deepways
Frewins
Shortwood Cl
Hooker Cl
Forge Cl
Bedland's Lane
Duke's Road
Queen's Rd
Barn
Knowle
Hgr Bedlands
St Peters CE Primary School
Leeford
KNOWLE HILL
B3178
EXMOUTH ROAD
SALTERTON ROAD
Knowle Road
Little Knowle
Dark Lane
Little Knowle
Lansdowne Road
Moorlands Road
Haise Hill La
West Hl Lane
WEST HILL
39
Quentance Farm
82
Castle Lane
Woodlands
Sherbrook Close
Sherbrook Hill
Fountain Hl
Road
Links Rd
East Devon Golf Club
Northview
South West Coast Path
Golf Course
81
Down
1 grid square represents 500 metres

EX9
Kersbrook
The Warren
South Farm
South Farm Road
Kersbrook Lane
Copp Hill La
BUDLEIGH EAST ROAD
B3178
Tidwell
Long Copp
Copp Hill Lane
Vision Hill Rd
Honey Pk Rd
Mansfield Ter
Warren Dr
Granary Lane
Bridge Road
Raleigh Rd
Vales Rd
Swains Rd
Stoneborough Lane
Leas Rd
Clarence Rd
Boyne Rd
Armytage Rd
Tidwell Close
Elmside
Westfield Cl
Westfield Rd
Stoneyford Pk
Cricket Field Lane
Barns Rd
Boucher Way
Boucher Road
Otter Ct
Ottervale Rd
Budleigh Salterton Hospital
Chapel Hill
Upper West Terrace
West Ter
The Lawn
Brook Rd
Chapel St
E Ter
FORE ST
FORE HILL
COASTGUARD ROAD
Salting Hl
CSTGRD HL
MARINE PDE
S PDE
HIGH STREET
FORE STREET
Queen St
Cliff Ter
Cliff Rd
Rolle Rd
Arden Close
Fairlynch Mus
South West Coast Path
Otterton Ledge
BUDLEIGH SALTERTON
E
F
G
H
07
08
83
82
81
1
2
3
4
5

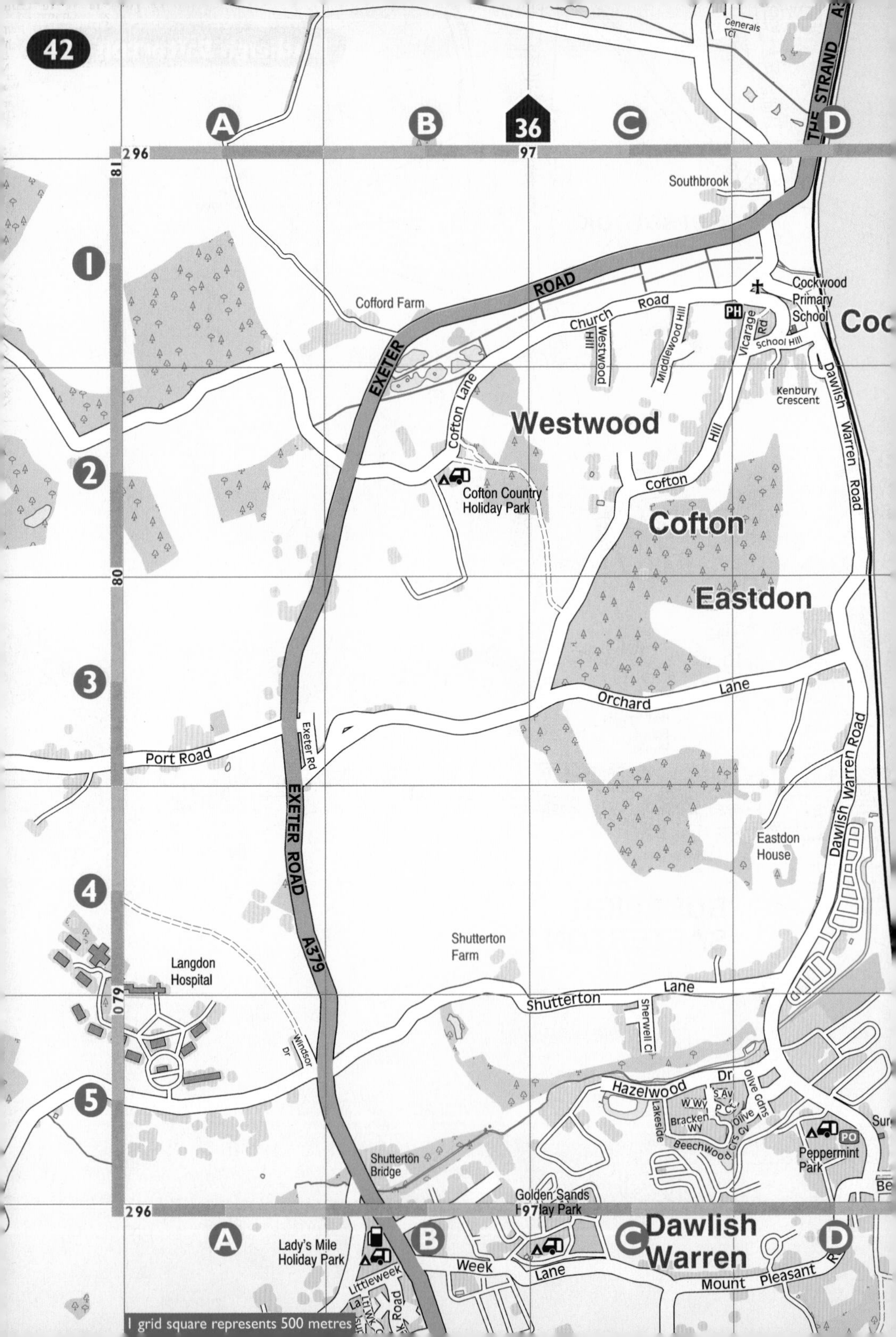

1 grid square represents 500 metres

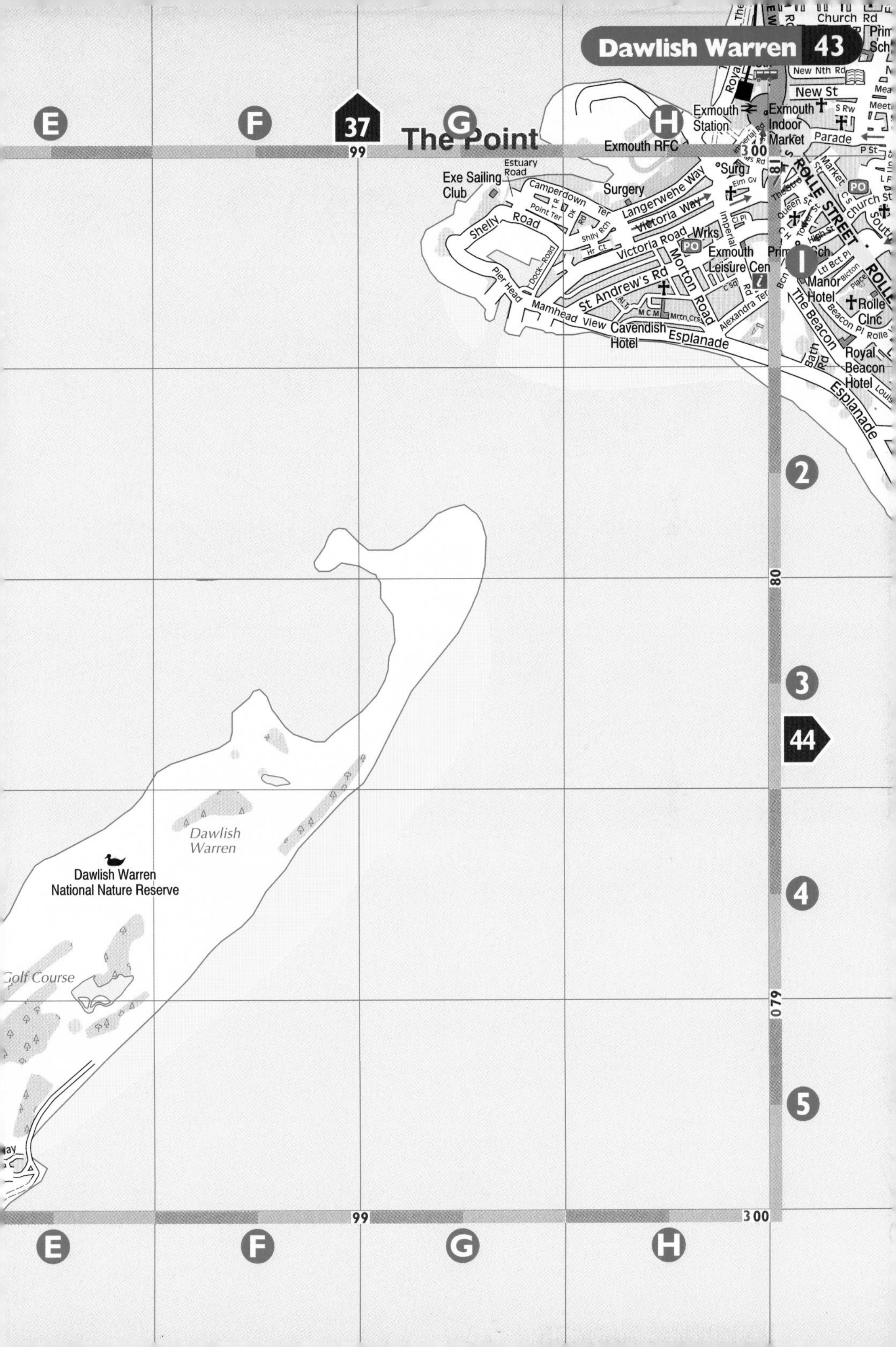

E
F
G
H
37
44
The Point
99
300
80
079
2
3
4
5
Exe Sailing Club
Estuary Road
Camperdown Ter
Point Ter
Shelly Road
Dock Road
Pier Head
Mamhead View
Cavendish Hotel
Esplanade
St Andrew's Rd
Victoria Road
Victoria Way
Langerwehe Way
Surgery
Surg
Wrks
PO
Morton Road
Imperial Rd
Alexandra Ter
Exmouth Leisure Cen
Exmouth RFC
Exmouth Station
Exmouth Indoor Market
Parade
New St
New Nth Rd
Church Rd
ROLLE STREET
Church St
Queen St
Tower St
High St
Market St
The Strd
Manor Hotel
The Beacon
Beacon Pl
Bath Rd
Royal Beacon Hotel
Rolle Clnc
Esplanade
Dawlish Warren
Dawlish Warren National Nature Reserve
Golf Course

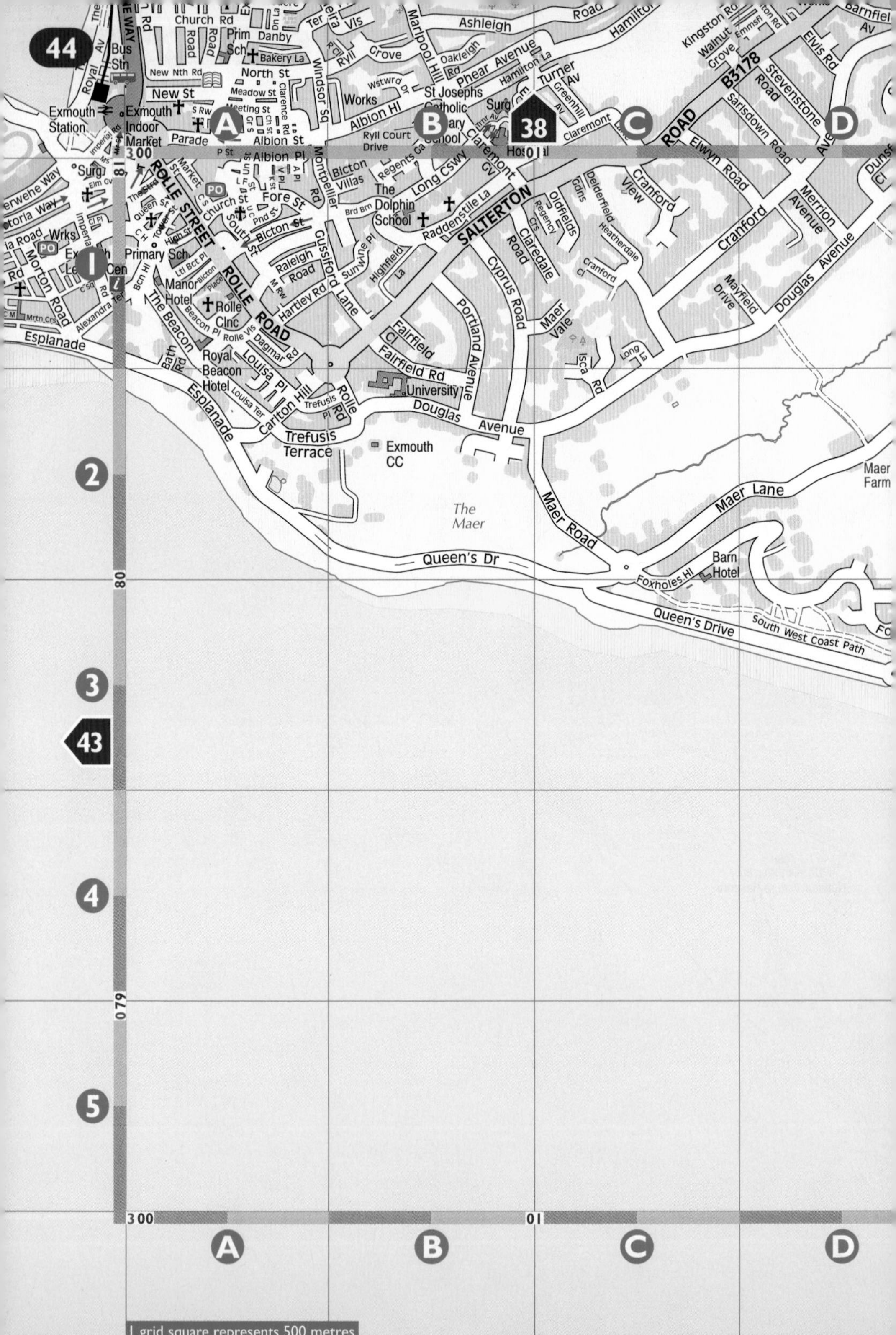

1 grid square represents 500 metres

Works
Littledown Close
Industrial Estate
Littleham CE Primary School
Littleham
Elm La
Woodlands Farm
St Margaret's Vw
Rodney Cl
39
E
F
G
H
03
04
Maer Lane
Down Lane
West Down Farm
The World of Country Life
Prattshayes Farm
Meadow Crescent
Devon Cliffs Holiday Park
West Down View
South West Coast Path
Works
Gore Lane
Gore Lane
Gore Lane
High Land of Orcombe
South West Coast Path
Sandy Bay
Straight Point
81
80
079
1
2
3
4
5
03
04
E
F
G
H

Alphington 20 A3
Blackhorse 10 D5
Broadclyst 5 H3
Budleigh Salterton 41 F4
Bystock 39 E1
Clyst Honiton 11 G5
Clyst St George 23 E4
Clyst St Mary 16 D5
Cockwood 42 D1
Cofton 42 C2
Countess Wear 21 F1
Cowley 7 E1
Dawlish Warren 42 C5
Duryard 7 H3
Eastdon 42 C3
Ebford 28 A1
Exeter 2 A5
Exminster 26 A3
Exmouth 38 B4
Exton 27 H4
Exwick 7 E5
Heavitree 15 E2
Hulham 38 B1
Huxham 4 B2
Ide 18 D2
Kenn 31 E1
Kennford 24 D5
Kenton 32 C5
Kersbrook 41 F1
Knowle 40 C2
Littleham 39 E5
Little Knowle 40 C3
Lower Wear 21 F4
Lympstone 34 A4
Markham Cross 18 D4
Marley Hayes 35 H4
Monkerton 10 A5
Nadderwater 6 C5
Pennsylvania 7 H4
Pinhoe 10 B3
The Point 37 G5
Polsloe 14 C1
Poltimore 5 F4
Powderham 33 F4
Ratsloe 4 D2
Redhills 13 E3
St Thomas 13 G5
Sandy Gate 16 B4
Shillingford Abbot 19 G5
Shillingford St George 24 B2
South Town 36 B2
Sowton 16 C2
Starcross
Stoke Canon
Stoke Hill
Topsham
Westwood
Whipton
Withycombe Raleigh
Wonford
Woodbury
Woodmanton

USING THE STREET INDEX

Street names are listed alphabetically. Each street name is followed by its postal town or area locality, the Postcode District, the page number, and the reference to the square in which the name is found.

Standard index entries are shown as follows:

Abbeville Cl *EXS* EX2 ....**14** C5

Street names and selected addresses not shown on the map due to scale restrictions are shown in the index with an asterisk:

Acland Ter *EXN* EX4 * **2** E1

GENERAL ABBREVIATIONS

ACC	ACCESS
ALY	ALLEY
AP	APPROACH
AR	ARCADE
ASS	ASSOCIATION
AV	AVENUE
BCH	BEACH
BLDS	BUILDINGS
BND	BEND
BNK	BANK
BR	BRIDGE
BRK	BROOK
BTM	BOTTOM
BUS	BUSINESS
BVD	BOULEVARD
BY	BYPASS
CATH	CATHEDRAL
CEM	CEMETERY
CEN	CENTRE
CFT	CROFT
CH	CHURCH
CHA	CHASE
CHYD	CHURCHYARD
CIR	CIRCLE
CIRC	CIRCUS
CL	CLOSE
CLFS	CLIFFS
CMP	CAMP
CNR	CORNER
CO	COUNTY
COLL	COLLEGE
COM	COMMON
COMM	COMMISSION
CON	CONVENT
COT	COTTAGE
COTS	COTTAGES
CP	CAPE
CPS	COPSE
CR	CREEK
CREM	CREMATORIUM
CRS	CRESCENT
CSWY	CAUSEWAY
CT	COURT
CTRL	CENTRAL
CTS	COURTS
CTYD	COURTYARD
CUTT	CUTTINGS
CV	COVE
CYN	CANYON
DEPT	DEPARTMENT
DL	DALE
DM	DAM
DR	DRIVE
DRO	DROVE
DRY	DRIVEWAY
DWGS	DWELLINGS
E	EAST
EMB	EMBANKMENT
EMBY	EMBASSY
ESP	ESPLANADE
EST	ESTATE
EX	EXCHANGE
EXPY	EXPRESSWAY
EXT	EXTENSION
F/O	FLYOVER
FC	FOOTBALL CLUB
FK	FORK
FLD	FIELD
FLDS	FIELDS
FLS	FALLS
FLS	FLATS
FM	FARM
FT	FORT
FWY	FREEWAY
FY	FERRY
GA	GATE
GAL	GALLERY
GDN	GARDEN
GDNS	GARDENS
GLD	GLADE
GLN	GLEN
GN	GREEN
GND	GROUND
GRA	GRANGE
GRG	GARAGE
GT	GREAT
GTWY	GATEWAY
GV	GROVE
HGR	HIGHER
HL	HILL
HLS	HILLS
HO	HOUSE
HOL	HOLLOW
HOSP	HOSPITAL
HRB	HARBOUR
HTH	HEATH
HTS	HEIGHTS
HVN	HAVEN
HWY	HIGHWAY
IMP	IMPERIAL
IN	INLET
IND EST	INDUSTRIAL ESTATE
INF	INFIRMARY
INFO	INFORMATION
INT	INTERCHANGE
IS	ISLAND
JCT	JUNCTION
JTY	JETTY
KG	KING
KNL	KNOLL
L	LAKE
LA	LANE
LDG	LODGE
LGT	LIGHT
LK	LOCK
LKS	LAKES
LNDG	LANDING
LTL	LITTLE
LWR	LOWER
MAG	MAGISTRATE
MAN	MANSIONS
MD	MEAD
MDW	MEADOWS
MEM	MEMORIAL
MKT	MARKET
MKTS	MARKETS
ML	MALL
ML	MILL
MNR	MANOR
MS	MEWS
MSN	MISSION
MT	MOUNT
MTN	MOUNTAIN
MTS	MOUNTAINS
MUS	MUSEUM
MWY	MOTORWAY
N	NORTH
NE	NORTH EAST
NW	NORTH WEST
O/P	OVERPASS
OFF	OFFICE
ORCH	ORCHARD
OV	OVAL
PAL	PALACE
PAS	PASSAGE
PAV	PAVILION
PDE	PARADE
PH	PUBLIC HOUSE
PK	PARK
PKWY	PARKWAY
PL	PLACE
PLN	PLAIN
PLNS	PLAINS
PLZ	PLAZA
POL	POLICE STATION
PR	PRINCE
PREC	PRECINCT
PREP	PREPARATORY
PRIM	PRIMARY
PROM	PROMENADE
PRS	PRINCESS
PRT	PORT
PT	POINT
PTH	PATH
PZ	PIAZZA
QD	QUADRANT
QU	QUEEN
QY	QUAY
R	RIVER
RBT	ROUNDABOUT
RD	ROAD
RDG	RIDGE
REP	REPUBLIC
RES	RESERVOIR
RFC	RUGBY FOOTBALL CLUB
RI	RISE
RP	RAMP
RW	ROW
S	SOUTH
SCH	SCHOOL
SE	SOUTH
SER	SERVICE
SH	
SHOP	SHO
SKWY	SK
SMT	SU
SOC	SO
SP	
SPR	S
SQ	SQ
ST	S
STN	ST
STR	ST
STRD	ST
SW	SOUTH
TDG	TR
TER	TE
THWY	THROUG
TNL	TU
TOLL	TOL
TPK	TUR
TR	
TRL	
TWR	T
U/P	UNDE
UNI	UNIV
UPR	
V	
VA	V
VIAD	VIA
VIL	
VIS	
VLG	V
VLS	
VW	
W	
WD	
WHF	W
WK	
WKS	
WLS	
WY	
YD	
YHA	YOUTH H

POSTCODE TOWNS AND AREA ABBREVIATIONS

BUD	Budleigh Salterton
DAW	Dawlish
EX	Exeter
EXM	Exmouth
EXN	Exeter north
EXS	Exeter south
REXNE	Rural Exeter north & east
REXSW	Rural Exeter south & west
TOP/EXT	Topsham/

Index - streets

A

Abbeville Cl *EXS* EX2 **14** C5
Abbey Ct *EXS* EX2 **16** B3
Abbey Rd *EXN* EX4 **8** D5
Abbot's Rd *EXN* EX4 **8** C5
Acland Rd *EXN* EX4 **2** D1
Acland Ter *EXN* EX4 * **2** E1
The Acorns *EXN* EX4 * **8** B3
Addington Ct *EXN* EX4 **14** A1
Addison Cl *EXN* EX4 **13** E2
Albany Cl *EXM* EX8 **39** E2
Albany Rd *EXS* EX2 **13** G4
Alberta Crs *EXN* EX4 **8** D4
Albert Pl *EXM* EX8 **44** A1
Albert St *EX* EX1 **3** F1
Albion Hl *EXM* EX8 **38** B5
Albion Pl *EXM* EX8 **44** A1
EXN EX4 **14** B1
Albion St *EXM* EX8 **38** A5
EXN EX4 **13** G3
Aldens Rd *EXS* EX2 **19** H3
Aldrin Rd *EXN* EX4 **8** B3
Alexandra Ter *EX* EX1 **14** C1
EXM EX8 **43** H1
Alford Cl *EX* EX1 **15** G1
Alford Crs *EX* EX1 **15** F1
Alfranza Cl *EX* EX1 * **15** F2
Allervale Cl *EXS* EX2 **15** F4
Allhallows Ct *EXN* EX4 **2** A4
Allington Md *EXN* EX4 **7** G3
Alpha St *EX* EX1 **3** K3
Alphin Brook Rd *EXS* EX2 **19** H2
Alphington Rd *EXS* EX2 **2** A7
Alphington St *EXN* EX4 **2** A5
Alston Ter *EXM* EX8 **43** H1
Altamira *TOP/EXT* EX3 **27** F1
Ambassador Dr *EX* EX1 **16** A1
Anne Cl *EXN* EX4 **8** C4
Anson Rd *EXM* EX8 **38** C2
Anthony Rd *EX* EX1 **3** K3
Antonine Crs *EXN* EX4 **13** E2
Apple Cl *EXM* EX8 **38** B1
Apple Farm Gra *EXS* EX2 **16** A5
Apple La *EXS* EX2 **16** A4
April Cl *EXM* EX8 **38** A1
The Arcade *EX* EX1 * **2** C2
Archibald Rd *EX* EX1 **2** E3
The Arch *REXNE* EX5 **29** F3
Arden Cl *BUD* EX9 **41** E4
Arena Pk *EXN* EX4 **9** F4
Argyll Ms *EXN* EX4 * **7** G4
Argyll Rd *EXN* EX4 **7** H3
Armstrong Av *EXN* EX4 **8** B3
Armytage Rd *BUD* EX9 **41** E2
Arthurs Cl *EXM* EX8 **38** D2
Arundel Cl *EXS* EX2 **19** H3
Ash Farm Cl *EX* EX1 **10** B4
Ashfield Cl *EXM* EX8 **39** E3
Ashford Rd *TOP/EXT* EX3 **27** E1
Ash Gv *EXM* EX8 **38** B2
Ashleigh *EXS* EX2 **19** G3
Ashleigh Cl *EXN* EX4 **13** F2
Ashleigh Mount Rd *EXN* EX4 **13** F3
Ashleigh Rd *EXM* EX8 **38** B5
Ashton Rd *EXS* EX2 **13** H5
Ashwood Rd *EXS* EX2 **13** H5
Aspen Cl *EXS* EX2 **15** G4
Athelstan Rd *EX* EX1 **2** E3
Atkinson Cl *EXN* EX4 **9** E5
Attwyll Av *EXS* EX2 **15** E3
Austen Cl *EXN* EX4 **9** G5
Avalon Cl *EXN* EX4 **9** E3
The Avenue *TOP/EXT* EX3 **28** A5
Avocet Rd *EXS* EX2 **16** B2
Avondale Rd *EXM* EX8 **38** D4
EXS EX2 **15** E3

B

Babblebrook Ms *EX* EX1 **10** B5
Badger Cl *EXS* EX2 **15** H3
Bad Homburg Wy *EXS* EX2 **20** B3
Badon Cl *EXN* EX4 **9** E3
Bagshot Av *EXS* EX2 **14** B5
Bailey St *EXN* EX4 **2** C2
Bakers Hl *REXSW* EX6 **12** C5
Baker St *EXS* EX2 **3** H4
Bakery La *EXM* EX8 **38** A5
Balls Farm Rd *EXS* EX2 **19** F1
Balmoral Gdns *TOP/EXT* EX3 **27** E1
Bampfylde St *EX* EX1 **2** E2
Bankside *EXM* EX8 **38** C1
Bapton Cl *EXM* EX8 **38** B3
Bapton La *EXM* EX8 **38** B3
Barbican Steps *EXN* EX4 **2** A4
Baring Crs *EX* EX1 **3** G3
Baring Ter *EXS* EX2 **2** D7
Barley Farm Rd *EXN* EX4 **13** E4
Barley La *EXN* EX4 **12** D2
Barley Mt *EXN* EX4 **13** E3
Barnardo Rd *EXS* EX2 **2** D6
Barnfield Av *EXM* EX8 **38** D5
Barnfield Crs *EX* EX1 * **2** D3
Barnfield Hl *EX* EX1 **2** E3
Barnfield Rd *EX* EX1 **2** E3
Barn La *BUD* EX9 **40** D2
Barns Rd *BUD* EX9 **41** F3
Barnstone Ct *EXS* EX2 **19** G3
Barrack La *EXS* EX2 **19** F5
Barrack Rd *EXS* EX2 **3** H4
Barrowdale Cl *EXM* EX8 **35** G5
Bartholomew St East *EXN* EX4 **2** A3
Bartholomew St West *EXN* EX4 **2** A4
Bartholomew Ter *EXN* EX4 * **2** A4
Barton Cl *TOP/EXT* EX3 **28** A4
Barton Hayes Ct *EXN* EX4 **13** G3
Barton La *EXS* EX2 **19** E5
Barton Ms *TOP/EXT* EX3 **28** A5
Barton Rd *EXS* EX2 **13** F5
Bassetts Gdns *EXM* EX8 **38** D2
Bate Cl *EXS* EX2 **19** G2
Bathern Rd *EXS* EX2 **15** H4
Bath Rd *EXM* EX8 **44** A2
Baxter Cl *EXS* EX2 **15** H5
Bay Trees *REXSW* EX6 **30** C1
Bazley Sq *EX* EX1 **10** A5
Beach Rd *DAW* EX7 **42** D5
Beacon Av *EXN* EX4 **8** D5
Beacon Heath *EXN* EX4 **9** F4
Beacon Hl *EXM* EX8
Beacon La *EXN* EX4
Beacon Pl *EXM* EX8
The Beacon *EXM* EX8
Bears' La *BUD* EX9
Bear St *EX* EX1
Beaufort Rd *EXS* EX2
Beaworthy Cl *EXS* EX2
Bedford St *EX* EX1
Bedland's La *BUD* EX9
Beech Av *EXN* EX4
Beeches Cl *REXNE* EX5
Beechway *EXM* EX8
Beechwood Crs *DAW* EX7
Belgrave Rd *EX* EX1
Belle Isle Dr *EXS* EX2
Belle Vue Cl *REXSW* EX6
Belle Vue Rd *EXM* EX8
EXN EX4
Belmont Rd *EX* EX1
Belvedere Cl *TOP/EXT* EX3
Belvedere Rd *EXM* EX8
Belvidere Rd *EXN* EX4
Bennett Cl *EXS* EX2
Bennett Sq *EXN* EX4
Berkshire Dr *EXN* EX4
Bernadette Cl *EXN* EX4
Berrybrook Meadow
REXSW EX6
Berry Cl *EXM* EX8
Betjemen Dr *EXM* EX8
Betony Ri *EXS* EX2
Bettys Md *EXN* EX4
Beverley Cl *EXS* EX2

C

D

E

F

Friars' Ga *EXS* EX2 2 C5
Friars' Wk *EXS* EX2 2 C5
Friernhay St *EXN* EX4 2 A4
Frobisher Rd *EXM* EX8 38 C2
Frog La *REXNE* EX5 16 C5
Frog St *EXN* EX4 2 A5
Fulford Rd *EX* EX1 14 D1
Fulford Wy *REXNE* EX5 29 G4
Furze Rd *REXNE* EX5 29 F3

G

Galahad Cl *EXN* EX4 9 E4
Galmpton Ri *EXN* EX4 8 C4
Galsworthy Sq *EXN* EX4 9 F5
Gandy St *EXN* EX4 2 B2
Garden Cl *EXS* EX2 15 G4
Gareth Crs *EXN* EX4 8 D3
Garland Cl *EXN* EX4 6 D5
Garratt Cl *EXM* EX8 38 C1
Gater La *EX* EX1 2 C4
Generals Cl *REXSW* EX6 36 C5
Generals La *REXSW* EX6 36 D5
Geneva Cl *EXS* EX2 3 H6
Georges Cl *EX* EX1 15 F2
George St *EX* EX1 2 B4
EXM EX8 38 A5
Gervase Av *EXS* EX2 2 A6
Gibraltar Rd *EXM* EX8 34 C3
Gibson Cl *EXM* EX8 39 E3
Gilbert Av *EXS* EX2 15 G4
Gipsy Hill La *EX* EX1 10 B5
Gipsy La *EXM* EX8 38 A4
Gissons *REXSW* EX6 26 B2
Gissons La *REXSW* EX6 30 D1
Gittisham Cl *EX* EX1 15 H2
Gladstone Rd *EX* EX1 3 G3
Glasshouse La *EXS* EX2 21 E3
Glastonbury Cl *EXN* EX4 9 E3
Glave Saunders Av
EXS EX2 15 G4
Glebe Cl *EXM* EX8 34 C3
Glebelands *EXM* EX8 34 C3
REXSW EX6 26 A2
Glen Cl *REXNE* EX5 23 G1
Glenmore Rd *EXS* EX2 15 E3
Glenthorne Rd *EXN* EX4 7 G4
Glenwood Ri *EXS* EX2 2 E7
Globefield *TOP/EXT* EX3 27 F1
Globe Hl *REXNE* EX5 29 F3
Globe La *TOP/EXT* EX3 27 F2
Gloucester Rd *EXM* EX8 38 D1
EXN EX4 13 E2
Goldsmith St *EX* EX1 3 J2
Good Shepherd Dr
EXS EX2 2 C5
Gordon Rd *EX* EX1 3 G1
TOP/EXT EX3 22 A5
Gordon's Pl *EXS* EX2 3 K4
Gore La *EXM* EX8 45 F2
Gorfin Evett Cl *EXM* EX8 39 E4
Gorse La *EXM* EX8 35 H5
Govetts *REXNE* EX5 29 G3
Grace Rd Central *EXS* EX2 20 A1
Grace Rd South *EXS* EX2 20 B2
Grace Rd West *EXS* EX2 19 H1
Grafton Rd *EXN* EX4 7 G4
Grainger Cl *EXS* EX2 15 G3
Granary La *BUD* EX9 41 G2
Grange Av *EXM* EX8 38 B3
Grange Cl *EXM* EX8 34 D4
EXM EX8 38 B4
Gras Lawn *EXS* EX2 14 C5
Grasslands Dr *EX* EX1 10 A5
Great Hill Vw *EXN* EX4 8 C2
Greatwood Ter
TOP/EXT EX3 27 E1
Grecian Wy *EXS* EX2 15 G4
Green Cl *EXM* EX8 38 C4
Greenhill Av *EXM* EX8 34 C4
EXM EX8 38 C5
Green La *EXN* EX4 13 E3
TOP/EXT EX3 27 H4
Greenpark Av *EX* EX1 15 H1
Greenpark Rd *EXM* EX8 38 D2
The Green *EXM* EX8 39 F5
EXS EX2 18 D2
Greenway *EXS* EX2 13 E5
REXNE EX5 29 G3
Greenway La *BUD* EX9 40 D2
Greenwood Dr *EXS* EX2 15 H3
Grenadier Rd *REXNE* EX5 16 A1
Grendon Rd *EX* EX1 3 H3
Grenville Av *EXN* EX4 9 G5
Grenville Rd *EXM* EX8 38 C2
Grindle Wy *REXNE* EX5 22 D1
Grosvenor Pl *EX* EX1 3 F1
Grove Hl *TOP/EXT* EX3 27 F1
Guildford Cl *EXN* EX4 13 E2
Guinea St *EX* EX1 2 B4
Guinevere Wy *EXN* EX4 9 E4
Guinness La *EXN* EX4 7 E5
Gussiford La *EXM* EX8 44 A1
Guys Rd *EXN* EX4 13 F2

H

Haccombe Cl *EXN* EX4 13 E3
Hadrian Dr *EXN* EX4 13 E2
Hadrians Wy *EXM* EX8 38 D3
Haldon Cl *TOP/EXT* EX3 22 A5
Haldon Rd *EXN* EX4 13 G2
Haldon View Ter *EXS* EX2 3 H5
Haley Cl *EXM* EX8 38 C2
Halscombe La *EXS* EX2 18 A3
Halsdon Av *EXM* EX8 38 A4
Halsdon La *EXM* EX8 38 A2
Halsdon Rd *EXM* EX8 38 A5
Halse Hill La *BUD* EX9 40 D3
Halses Cl *EXN* EX4 6 D5
Halyards *EXM* EX8 * 43 G1
Hambeer La *EXS* EX2 13 E5
Hamilton Av *EXS* EX2 20 D1
Hamilton Dr *EXS* EX2 15 H3
Hamilton Gv *REXSW* EX6 36 D5
Hamilton La *EXM* EX8 38 C5
Hamilton Rd *EXM* EX8 38 D5
TOP/EXT EX3 22 A5
Hamlin Gdns *EX* EX1 15 E1
Hamlin La *EX* EX1 15 E2
Hammond Croft Wy *EXS* EX2 19 H3
Hampden Pl *EXS* EX2 * 2 A6
Hampshire Cl *EXN* EX4 13 E4
The Hams *EXS* EX2 18 D2
Hanover Cl *EX* EX1 3 J2
Hanover Rd *EX* EX1 3 J2
Harbour Ct *EXM* EX8 43 H1
Hardy Rd *EXS* EX2 15 H3
Harebell Copse *EXN* EX4 6 D5
Harefield Cl *EXN* EX4 7 G5
Harefield Dr *EXM* EX8 34 D4
Harefield Rd *EXM* EX8 35 E3
Harrier Wy *EXS* EX2 16 A4
Harringcourt Rd *EXN* EX4 10 A3
Harrington Dr *EXN* EX4 10 A3
Harrington Gdns *EXN* EX4 10 A4
Harrington La *EXN* EX4 9 H3
Hartley Rd *EXM* EX8 44 A1
Hartopp Rd *EXM* EX8 38 A5
Harts Cl *EX* EX1 10 A5
Hart's La *EX* EX1 9 H5
Harwood Cl *EXM* EX8 38 D3
Hatchland Rd *EXN* EX4 5 F4
Hatherleigh Rd *EXS* EX2 19 G1
Haven Banks *EXS* EX2 2 C6
Haven Cl *EXS* EX2 2 B7
Haven Rd *EXS* EX2 2 A6
Hawthorn Gv *EXM* EX8 39 E2
Hawthorn Rd *EXS* EX2 14 D5
Hawthorn Wy *EXS* EX2 19 G3
Hayes Cl *BUD* EX9 41 E2
Hayne Cl *EXN* EX4 15 E1
Haynes La *REXSW* EX6 18 A1
Haytor Dr *EXN* EX4 7 E5
Hazeldene Gdns *EXM* EX8 38 A3
Hazelmead Rd *REXNE* EX5 23 G1
Hazel Rd *EXS* EX2 20 D1
Hazelwood Dr *DAW* EX7 42 C5
Headland Cl *EX* EX1 15 G1
Headland Crs *EX* EX1 15 G1
Headon Gdns *EXS* EX2 21 E2
Heard Av *EXM* EX8 39 E4
Heather Cl *EX* EX1 15 F2
Heatherdale *EXM* EX8 44 C1
Heath Rd *EXS* EX2 15 F4
Heavitree Pk *EXS* EX2 15 E3
Heavitree Rd *EX* EX1 3 F3
Hele Rd *EXN* EX4 13 G1
Heneaton Sq *EXS* EX2 21 F3
Henley Rd *EXM* EX8 38 C5
Hennock Rd Central *EXS* EX2 20 A2
Hennock Rd East *EXS* EX2 20 A2
Hennock Rd North *EXS* EX2 20 A1
Hensleigh Dr *EXS* EX2 3 G4
Herbert Rd *EX* EX1 14 D1
Hereford Cl *EXM* EX8 35 H5
Heron Rd *EXS* EX2 16 A3
Herschell Rd *EXN* EX4 8 C5
Hexworthy Av *EXN* EX4 7 E5
Heywood Dr *REXSW* EX6 36 C4
Highbury Pk *EXM* EX8 38 A3
Highcliffe Cl *EXM* EX8 34 B5
Highcroft *EXN* EX4 7 G4
Highcross Rd *EXN* EX4 14 A1
Higher Aboveway *REXSW* EX6 26 B3
Higher Barley Mt *EXN* EX4 13 E3
Higher Bedlands *BUD* EX9 40 D2
Higher Duryard *EXN* EX4 * 8 A3
Higher Hoopern La *EXN* EX4 8 B3
Higher King's Av *EXN* EX4 8 B4
Higher Shapter St
TOP/EXT EX3 27 F2
Higher Summerlands *EX* EX1 * 3 F2
Higher Wear Rd *EXS* EX2 21 G4
Highfield *TOP/EXT* EX3 22 B4
Highfield La *EXM* EX8 44 B1
High Mdw *EXN* EX4 13 E3
High St *BUD* EX9 41 E4
EXM EX8 44 A1
EXN EX4 2 C3
EXS EX2 18 D2
TOP/EXT EX3 22 A5
Hill Barton Cl *EX* EX1 15 G1
Hill Barton La *EX* EX1 15 G1
Hill Barton Rd *EX* EX1 15 G1
Hill Cl *EXN* EX4 8 B4
Hill Crest *REXSW* EX6 26 A2
Hillcrest Pk *EXN* EX4 8 A3
Hill Dr *EXM* EX8 38 B1
Hill La *EX* EX1 15 F1
EXN EX4 9 F5
Hill Ri *EX* EX1 15 G1
Hillsborough Av *EXN* EX4 14 A1
Hillside Av *EXN* EX4 14 A1
Hillyfield Rd *EX* EX1 15 G1
Hoker Rd *EXS* EX2 15 E4
Holland Rd *EXM* EX8 38 D3
EXS EX2 13 F4
Holley Cl *REXSW* EX6 26 A2
Holloway St *EXS* EX2 2 D5
Hollow La *EX* EX1 15 H1
Hollow Pits Ct *EXS* EX2 19 H3
The Hollows *EXM* EX8 38 B5
Hollymount Cl *EXM* EX8 38 C1
Holly Rd *EXS* EX2 14 D5
Holly Wk *EXM* EX8 38 D1
Holman Wy *TOP/EXT* EX3 27 F2
Holne Ct *EXN* EX4 * 7 E5
Holne Ri *EXS* EX2 15 F4
Homefield Rd *EX* EX1 3 J3
Honeylands Dr *EX* EX1 15 E1
Honeylands Wy *EX* EX1 15 E1
Honey La *EX* EX1 10 B3
Honey Park Rd *BUD* EX9 41 F2
Honeysuckle Ct *EXN* EX4 6 D5
Honiton Rd *EX* EX1 15 G3
REXNE EX5 16 C1
Hooker Cl *BUD* EX9 40 D2
Hoopern Av *EXN* EX4 8 A4
Hoopern La *EXN* EX4 8 A5
Hoopern St *EXN* EX4 13 H1
Hope Pl *EXS* EX2 * 15 E3
Hope Rd *EXS* EX2 15 E3
Horseguards *EXN* EX4 14 A1
Hospital La *EX* EX1 9 G5
Howard Cl *EXN* EX4 7 F5
Howell Rd *EXN* EX4 13 H1
Hulham Rd *EXM* EX8 38 B3
Hulham V *EXM* EX8 38 C2
Hummingbird Cl *EX* EX1 10 A4
Hunton Cl *EXM* EX8 34 C4
Hurst Av *EXS* EX2 15 F4
Hutchings Md *EX* EX1 10 B4
Hylton Gdns *EXN* EX4 13 F2

I

Iddesleigh Rd *EXN* EX4 8 C5
Ide La *EXS* EX2 19 H3
Ilex Cl *EXN* EX4 9 F3
EXS EX2 24 A2
Imperial Rd *EXM* EX8 37 H5
Imperial St *EXN* EX4 13 E3
Inner Ting Tong *BUD* EX9 40 A1
Iolanthe Dr *EXN* EX4 9 E3
Iona Av *EXM* EX8 38 A2
Iris Av *EXS* EX2 2 A6
Iron Br *EXN* EX4 2 A2
Isambard Pde *EXN* EX4 13 G1
Isca Rd *EXM* EX8 44 C1
EXS EX2 2 B7
Isleworth Rd *EXN* EX4 13 E3
Ivy Cl *EXS* EX2 15 E4
Ivydale *EXM* EX8 38 D1

J

James Owen Ct *EXN* EX4 14 B1
Jarvis Cl *EXM* EX8 38 D5
Jennifer Cl *EXS* EX2 14 C5
Jesmond Rd *EX* EX1 14 C1
Jocelyn Rd *BUD* EX9 41 E2
John Levers Wy *EXN* EX4 13 F2
John St *EXN* EX4 2 B4
Jubilee Cl *REXSW* EX6 26 B2
Jubilee Dr *EXM* EX8 38 C1
Jubilee Rd *EXN* EX4 14 C1
Juniper Cl *EXN* EX4 9 F3
Jupes Cl *REXSW* EX6 26 B3

K

Kay Cl *EXM* EX8 38 C4
Keats Cl *EXM* EX8 35 G5
Kenbury Crs *REXSW* EX6 42 D2
Kenbury Dr *EXS* EX2 20 A3
Kendall Cl *EXN* EX4 * 14 B1
Kennerley Av *EXN* EX4 9 F5
Kennford Rd *EXS* EX2 13 H5
Kenn La *REXSW* EX6 25 H5
Kent Cl *EXS* EX2 15 E4
Kersbrook La *BUD* EX9 41 E1
Kerswill Rd *EXN* EX4 13 F4
Kestor Dr *EXN* EX4 7 E5
Kestrel Wy *EXS* EX2 16 A3
Keverel Rd *EXM* EX8 38 A3
Kilb Arran Ri *EXN* EX4 7 G5
Kimberley Rd *EXS* EX2 2 D5
King Arthur's Rd *EXN* EX4 8 D3
Kingdom Ms *EXN* EX4 13 G1
King Edward St *EXN* EX4 7 G4
Kingfisher Dr *EXN* EX4 8 B3
King Henry's Rd *EXS* EX2 20 C1
Kingsgate *EXN* EX4 * 8 B5
Kingslake Ri *EXM* EX8 * 38 A4
Kingsley Av *EXN* EX4 9 F5
King's Rd *EXN* EX4 8 C5
Kingstephen Cl *EXN* EX4 14 A1
Kingston Rd *EXM* EX8 38 C5
King St *EXM* EX8 44 A1
EXN EX4 2 B4
Kingsway *EXS* EX2 3 K5
Kingswood Cl *EXN* EX4 7 E5
King William St *EXN* EX4 2 D1
Kinnerton Wy *EXN* EX4 6 D5
Kipling Dr *EXS* EX2 3 K7
Knightley Rd *EXS* EX2 14 C5
Knights Crs *EXS* EX2 15 H5
Knowle Dr *EXN* EX4 13 F1
Knowle Hl *BUD* EX9 40 B3
Knowle Rd *BUD* EX9 40 C2

L

Laburnum Cl *EXM* EX8 38 D1
Laburnum Rd *EXS* EX2 14 D5
Lackaborough Ct *EXS* EX2 19 G3
Ladysmith Rd *EX* EX1 3 J1
Lakelands Dr *EXN* EX4 13 F3
Lakeside *DAW* EX7 42 C5
Lakeside Av *EXS* EX2 21 F3
Lamacraft Dr *EXN* EX4 15 E1
Lamplough Rd *EXM* EX8 38 A1
Lancaster Cl *EXS* EX2 15 F4
Lancelot Rd *EXN* EX4 9 E3
Landhayes Rd *EXN* EX4 13 F3
Landscore Rd *EXN* EX4 13 F3
Lands Rd *EXN* EX4 9 H4
Langaton Gdns *EX* EX1 10 B4
Langaton La *EX* EX1 10 C5
Langerwehe Wy *EXM* EX8 43 H1
Langstone Dr *EXM* EX8 38 C2
Lansdowne *EXS* EX2 * 15 F4
Lansdowne Rd *BUD* EX9 40 B3
Lansdowne Ter *EXS* EX2 2 D5
Larch Cl *EXM* EX8 38 C1
Larch Rd *EXS* EX2 13 F5
Larkbeare Rd *EXS* EX2 2 D6
Lark Cl *EXN* EX4 8 B4
Latimer Rd *EXN* EX4 9 E5
Laurel Ri *EXM* EX8 38 D4
Laurel Rd *EXS* EX2 14 D5
Lavender Rd *EXN* EX4 7 E5
Lawn Rd *EXM* EX8 38 A5
The Lawn *BUD* EX9 41 E4
Lawrence Av *EXN* EX4 13 G3
Laxton Av *EX* EX1 15 G2
Leas Rd *BUD* EX9 41 E3
Lebanon Cl *EXN* EX4 8 C4
Legion Wy *EXS* EX2 19 H2
Leicester Md *EXN* EX4 13 E1
Leighdene Cl *EXS* EX2 3 G6
Leighton Ter *EXN* EX4 2 D1
Leslie Rd *EXM* EX8 38 A4
Lestock Cl *EXM* EX8 39 E5
Lethbridge Rd *EXS* EX2 15 F3
Lewis Crs *EXS* EX2 15 H5
Leypark Cl *EX* EX1 15 G1
Leypark Crs *EX* EX1 15 G2
Leypark Rd *EX* EX1 15 G1
Lichfield Rd *EXN* EX4 12 D2
Lichgate Rd *EXS* EX2 19 H3
Liffey Ri *EXN* EX4 7 E5
Lilac Rd *EXS* EX2 14 D5
Lily Mt *EXN* EX4 6 D5
Lime Gv *EXM* EX8 38 C1
REXSW EX6 26 A1
Limegrove Rd *EXN* EX4 13 F3
Lime Kiln La *EXS* EX2 21 E2
Lime Tree Cl *EXS* EX2 15 G5
Lincoln Cl *EXM* EX8 35 H5
Lincoln Rd *EXN* EX4 13 E2
Linda Cl *EX* EX1 15 G3
Linden Cl *EXM* EX8 38 C2
Linden V *EXN* EX4 * 13 H1
Linfield Gdns *EXN* EX4 13 F4
Links Rd *BUD* EX9 40 C4
Linnet Cl *EXN* EX4 8 B3
Lisa Cl *EXS* EX2 15 E4
Lister Cl *EXS* EX2 3 H7
Little Bicton Pl *EXM* EX8 44 A1
Littledown Cl *EXM* EX8 39 F5
Littleham Rd *EXM* EX8 39 E5
Little John's Cross Hl *EXS* EX2 13 E5
Little Knowle *BUD* EX9 40 D3
Littlemead La *EXM* EX8 38 A1
Little Meadow *EXM* EX8 38 D1
Little Queen St *EXN* EX4 2 C3
Little Rack St *EX* EX1 2 B4
Little Silver *EXN* EX4 2 A2
Little Silver La *EXS* EX2 25 F1
Littleway *EXS* EX2 13 F5
Liverton Cl *EXM* EX8 39 E4
Lloyds Ct *EX* EX1 9 G5
Lloyds Crs *EX* EX1 15 G1
Locarno Rd *EXN* EX4 13 E4
Locksley Cl *EXS* EX2 21 E3
Lodge Hl *EXN* EX4 7 G5
Longbrook La *EXM* EX8 34 D5
Longbrook St *EXN* EX4 2 D1
Longbrook Ter *EXN* EX4 2 C1
Long Cswy *EXM* EX8 44 B1
Long Copp *BUD* EX9 41 E2
Longdown Rd *REXSW* EX6 12 B5
Longfield Est *REXSW* EX6 36 C4
Long La *EXM* EX8 44 C1
Longmeadow *REXNE* EX5 29 G3
Longmeadow Rd *EXM* EX8 34 D4
Long Pk *REXNE* EX5 29 G3
Lonsdale Rd *EX* EX1 15 E3
Looe Rd *EXN* EX4 13 G1
Loram Wy *EXS* EX2 20 A3
Lords Wy *EXS* EX2 15 G4
Louisa Pl *EXM* EX8 44 A1
Louisa Ter *EXM* EX8 44 A2
Lovelace Crs *EXM* EX8 38 C4
Lovelace Gdns *EXS* EX2 19 H3
Lovell Cl *EXM* EX8 38 C1
Lovering Cl *EXM* EX8 38 C1
Lower Albert St *EX* EX1 3 F2
Lower Argyll Rd *EXN* EX4 7 G4
Lower Av *EX* EX1 3 J2
Lower Coombe St *EXS* EX2 2 B5
Lower Duck St *REXSW* EX6 26 B3
Lower Fore St *EXM* EX8 44 A1
Lower Harrington La *EXN* EX4 10 A4
Lower Hill Barton Rd *EX* EX1 15 G2
Lower King's Av *EXN* EX4 8 B5
Lower La *TOP/EXT* EX3 28 A2
Lower North St *EXN* EX4 2 A2
Lower St German's Rd *EXN* EX4 8 A5
Lower Shapter St *TOP/EXT* EX3 27 F2
Lower Summerlands *EX* EX1 3 F2
Lower Wear Rd *EXS* EX2 21 F3
Lucas Av *EXN* EX4 8 B5
Lucky La *EXS* EX2 2 C5
Ludwell La *EXS* EX2 15 F5
Lumley Cl *REXSW* EX6 36 A1
Lustleigh Cl *EXS* EX2 20 A3
Lymeborne Av *EX* EX1 15 E2
Lyncombe Cl *EXN* EX4 8 C4
Lyndhurst Rd *EXM* EX8 38 A4
EXS EX2 3 G5
Lynwood Av *EXN* EX4 13 G3

M

Madagascar Cl *EXM* EX8 39 E4
Madeira Vls *EXM* EX8 38 A5
Madison Av *EX* EX1 15 E2
Maer La *EXM* EX8 44 C2
Maer Rd *EXM* EX8
Maer V *EXM* EX8
Magdalen Gdns *EXS* EX2 *
Magdalen Rd *EX* EX1
Magdalen St *EX* EX1
Magnolia Av *EXM* EX8
EXS EX2
Main Rd *EX* EX1
Mallard Rd *EXS* EX2
Mallison Cl *EXN* EX4
Malt Fld *EXM* EX8
Malvern Gdns *EXS* EX2
Mamhead Rd *EXS* EX2
Mamhead Vw *EXM* EX8
Manaton Cl *EXS* EX2
Manchester Rd *EXM* EX8
Manchester St *EXM* EX8
Mandrake Cl *EXS* EX2
Mandrake Rd *EXS* EX2
Manor Pk *REXNE* EX5
Manor Rd *EXN* EX4
Mansfield Rd *EXN* EX4
Mansfield Ter *BUD* EX9
Manston Rd *EX* EX1
Manston Ter *EXS* EX2
Manstree Rd *EXS* EX2
Maple Dr *EXM* EX8
Maple Ms *BUD* EX9 *
Maple Rd *EXN* EX4
Marcom Cl *EXM* EX8
Marcus Rd *EXM* EX8
Mardon Hl *EXN* EX4
Margaret Rd *EXN* EX4
Marine Pde *BUD* EX9
Marine Wy *EXM* EX8
Marions Wy *EXM* EX8
Maristow Av *EXM* EX8
Market St *EX* EX1
EXM EX8
Markham La *EXS* EX2
Marlborough Cl *EXM* EX8
Marlborough Rd *EXS* EX2
The Marles *EXM* EX8
Marley Dr *EXM* EX8
Marley Rd *EXM* EX8
Marlpool Hl *EXM* EX8
Marpool Crs *EXM* EX8
Marpool Hl *EXM* EX8
Marsh Barton Rd *EXS* EX2
Marsh Green Rd East *EXS* EX2
Marsh Green Rd North *EXS* EX2
Marsh Green Rd West *EXS* EX2
Marsh La *TOP/EXT* EX3
Martins Rd *EXM* EX8
Mary Arches St *EXN* EX4
Maryfield Av *EXN* EX4
Marypole Rd *EXN* EX4
Masefield Rd *EXN* EX4
Masey Rd *EXM* EX8
Matford Av *EXS* EX2
Matford La *EXS* EX2
Matford Ms *EXS* EX2 *
Matford Park Rd *EXS* EX2
Matford Rd *EXS* EX2
Matthews Ct *EXN* EX4
Mayfield Dr *EXM* EX8
Mayfield Rd *EXN* EX4
EXS EX2
Mayflower Av *EXN* EX4
May St *EXN* EX4
Meadow Cl *EXM* EX8
REXNE EX5
Meadow Crs *EXM* EX8
Meadow Rd *BUD* EX9
Meadow St *EXM* EX8
Meadow Vw *EXM* EX8 *
Meadowview Rd *EXM* EX8
Meadow Wy *EXS* EX2
The Mede *EXN* EX4
TOP/EXT EX3
Medieval Br *EXN* EX4
Meeting La *EXM* EX8
Meeting St *EXM* EX8
Melbourne Pl *EXS* EX2
Melbourne St *EXS* EX2
Membury Cl *EX* EX1
Mercer Ct *EXS* EX2 *
Merlin Crs *EXN* EX4
Mermaid Yd *EX* EX1
Merrion Av *EXM* EX8
Merrivale Rd *EXN* EX4
Michigan Wy *EXN* EX4
Middlewood Hl *REXSW* EX6
Midway *EXM* EX8
Midway Cl *EXS* EX2
Milbury Cl *REXSW* EX6
Milbury La *REXSW* EX6
Mildmay Cl *EXN* EX4
Mile Gdns *EXN* EX4
Mile La *EXN* EX4
Millbrook La *EXS* EX2
Miller Cl *EXS* EX2
Miller Wy *REXSW* EX6
Milletts Cl *REXSW* EX6
Mill La *EXS* EX2
EXS EX2
REXNE EX5
TOP/EXT EX3
Mill Rd *EXS* EX2
Millside *EXS* EX2
Milton Cl *EXM* EX8
Milton Rd *EXS* EX2
Mincinglake Rd *EXN* EX4
The Mint *EXN* EX4 *
Mirey La *REXNE* EX5
Mitre La *EXN* EX4
Modred Cl *EXN* EX4
Monitor Cl *EXS* EX2
Monkerton Cl *EX* EX1
Monkerton Dr *EX* EX1
Monk's Rd *EXN* EX4
Monkswell Rd *EXN* EX4
Monmouth Av *TOP/EXT* EX3
Monmouth Hl *TOP/EXT* EX3
Monmouth St *TOP/EXT* EX3
Montague Ri *EXN* EX4

Le Grand *EX* EX1 3 H3
pellier Rd *EXM* EX8 38 A5
Hill Cl *EXS* EX2 20 A3
edge La *REXNE* EX5 5 H1
field Cl *EXM* EX8 38 C4
field Rd *EXM* EX8 38 C4
haven *BUD* EX9 40 D2
ands Rd *BUD* EX9 40 B3
and Wy *EXN* EX4 7 E5
La *BUD* EX9 40 D2
V EX4 5 F3
S EX2 16 A2
mead *BUD* EX9 40 D3
Pk *EXM* EX8 * 44 C1
view Cl *EXN* EX4 8 B4
y Rd *EXN* EX4 8 C5
mer Ct *EXS* EX2 * 21 E1
n Crs *EXM* EX8 43 H1
n Crescent Ms *EXM* EX8 43 H1
n Rd *EXM* EX8 43 H1
en Dr *EXM* EX8 38 A2
hayne La *EX* EX1 10 D2
XNE EX5 11 E5
tain Cl *EXM* EX8 39 F4
tbatten Cl *EXM* EX8 38 D2
t Dinham *EXN* EX4 * 13 G2
t Pleasant Av *EXM* EX8 38 B1
t Pleasant Rd *EXN* EX4 8 C5
t Radford Crs *EXS* EX2 2 E5
t Ri *REXSW* EX6 31 E2
t Wear Sq *EXS* EX2 21 F3
bray Av *EXN* EX4 2 D1
ank La *EXM* EX8 38 A4
erry Cl *EX* EX1 15 F2
rave Rw *EXN* EX4 2 C2
e Cl *EXS* EX2 19 H2
e Rd *EXN* EX4 13 E4
e Rw *EXM* EX8 44 A1

N

er Bottom *EXN* EX4 6 A5
er Park Rd *EXN* EX4 12 D3
ith Cl *EXM* EX8 38 D3
n Cl *TOP/EXT* EX3 27 E1
n Dr *EXM* EX8 39 E4
n Rd *EXN* EX4 13 G4
Bridge St *EXN* EX4 2 A5
ombe St *EX* EX1 3 K3
ombe Ter *EX* EX1 * 3 K3
ourt Rd *TOP/EXT* EX3 22 A4
oundland Cl *EXN* EX4 8 B3
ayes Cl *EXS* EX2 19 G1
ands Av *EXM* EX8 38 D3
ands Cl *EXS* EX2 19 G1
han Ct *EXN* EX4 13 E3
han Rd *EXN* EX4 13 F3
North Rd *EXM* EX8 38 A5
V EX4 2 C1
ort Rd *EXS* EX2 21 G4
Rd *REXSW* EX6 36 C4
St *EXM* EX8 38 A5
own Cl *EX* EX1 * 3 F2
Valley Rd *EXN* EX4 13 F1
las Rd *EX* EX1 15 E2
an Cl *EXM* EX8 38 D2
an Crs *BUD* EX9 41 E2
andy Cl *EXM* EX8 39 E3
andy Rd *EX* EX1 3 K3
Av *EX* EX1 3 H2
brook Cl *EXN* EX4 9 E4
ernhay Pl *EXN* EX4 2 C2
ernhay Sq *EXN* EX4 2 B2
ernhay St *EXN* EX4 2 B3
Lawn Ct *EX* EX1 3 K2
Park Rd *EXN* EX4 7 H4
St *EX* EX1 3 K3
M EX8 38 A5
V EX4 2 B3
P/EXT EX3 27 F2
view Rd *BUD* EX9 40 D4
ch Cl *EXM* EX8 35 H5
ch Rd *EXN* EX4 13 E2
ood Av *EXS* EX2 2 E7
ries Cl *TOP/EXT* EX3 22 A5
P/EXT EX3 28 A5
ry Cl *EXM* EX8 38 C4
ry Ms *EXM* EX8 38 C4
ook *EXM* EX8 38 B3
ell Rd *EXM* EX8 34 C3

O

EX EX1 * 3 K4
V EX4 10 A4
S EX2 19 G5
XSW EX6 26 A2
eld Rd *EXN* EX4 13 G3
eld St *EX* EX1 3 J4
ayes Rd *REXNE* EX5 29 F3
gh Rd *EXM* EX8 38 B5
y Cl *EX* EX1 10 A4
dge *EXS* EX2 19 G3
d *EXN* EX4 13 F4
ee Cl *EXM* EX8 38 B1
ood Ri *EXM* EX8 39 E1
La *REXNE* EX5 23 E1
ampton Pl *EXN* EX4 13 G3
ampton Rd *EXN* EX4 13 F3
ampton St *EXN* EX4 13 G3
bbey Ct *EXS* EX2 14 C5
akery Cl *EXN* EX4 13 F1
vstock Dr *EXM* EX8 39 E1
awlish Rd *REXSW* EX6 24 D4
ford La *TOP/EXT* EX3 28 A2
ds *EXM* EX8 44 C1
e La *EXS* EX2 19 E1
arket Cl *EXS* EX2 * 13 H5
atford La *EXS* EX2 20 B4
ll Cl *EXS* EX2 2 E7

Old Park Rd *EXN* EX4 2 D1
Old Pavilion Cl *EXS* EX2 15 G4
Old Pinn La *EX* EX1 10 A4
Old Rydon Cl *EXS* EX2 22 A1
Old Rydon La *EXS* EX2 21 H2
Old Rydon Ley *EXS* EX2 21 H2
Old's Vw *EXN* EX4 13 G1
Old Tiverton Rd *EXN* EX4 14 B1
Old Vicarage Cl *EXS* EX2 18 D2
Old Vicarage Rd *EXS* EX2 13 G4
Olive Gdns *DAW* EX7 42 D5
Olive Gv *DAW* EX7 42 D5
Orchard Cl *EX* EX1 10 B4
EXM EX8 34 C4
EXM EX8 38 A3
REXNE EX5 29 G3
Orchard Gdns *EXS* EX2 13 F4
Orchard Hl *EXS* EX2 13 E5
Orchard La *DAW* EX7 42 C3
Orchard Vw *EX* EX1 * 3 K4
Orchard Wy *TOP/EXT* EX3 27 E1
Oriole Dr *EXN* EX4 8 B4
Orwell Garth *EXN* EX4 9 G4
Osprey Rd *REXNE* EX5 16 B2
Otter Ct *BUD* EX9 41 G3
Otter Reach *BUD* EX9 * 41 F2
Ottervale Rd *BUD* EX9 41 G3
Outer Ting Tong *BUD* EX9 39 H1
Oxford Rd *EXN* EX4 2 E1
Oxford St *EXS* EX2 13 G4

P

Painters Ct *EXS* EX2 2 B6
Palace Ga *EX* EX1 2 C4
Palm Cl *EXM* EX8 38 D1
Palm Ct *DAW* EX7 42 C5
Palmer Ms *BUD* EX9 * 41 E4
Palmerston Dr *EXN* EX4 13 E1
Pamela Rd *EXN* EX4 14 D1
Pankhurst Cl *EXM* EX8 39 E5
The Panney *EX* EX1 15 E1
Parade *EXM* EX8 38 A5
Paris St *EXN* EX4 2 D2
Paris Street Ar *EX* EX1 * 2 D2
Park Cl *EXN* EX4 8 B3
REXNE EX5 29 G4
Parkers Cross La *EX* EX1 10 B3
Parker's Rd *REXSW* EX6 36 C4
Parkfield Rd *TOP/EXT* EX3 27 F1
Parkhouse Rd *EXS* EX2 13 F5
Parkland Dr *EXS* EX2 15 G5
Park La *BUD* EX9 40 D3
EXM EX8 38 A4
EXN EX4 10 A2
Park Pl *EX* EX1 3 J3
EXS EX2 3 F5
Park Rd *EX* EX1 3 H1
EXM EX8 38 A4
Parkside Crs *EX* EX1 10 B2
Parkside Dr *EXM* EX8 38 D2
Parkside Rd *EX* EX1 10 B2
Park Vw *EXM* EX8 * 35 E4
Park Wy *EXM* EX8 38 C4
Parkway *EXS* EX2 13 F5
Park Wy *REXNE* EX5 29 G4
Parr Cl *EX* EX1 * 3 F1
Parr St *EX* EX1 3 F1
Parsonage Wy *REXNE* EX5 29 G3
Parson Cl *EXM* EX8 38 C2
Parthia Pl *EXM* EX8 39 E3
Partridge Rd *EXM* EX8 38 C2
Patricia Cl *EXN* EX4 8 A3
Paul St *EXN* EX4 2 B3
Pavilion Pl *EX* EX1 2 D4
Paynes Ct *EXN* EX4 * 9 F5
Peel Rw *EX* EX1 * 9 G5
Pellinore Rd *EXN* EX4 9 E4
Pendragon Rd *EXN* EX4 8 D3
Penhayes Rd *REXSW* EX6 36 A1
Peninsula Pk *EXS* EX2 * 15 G4
Penlee *BUD* EX9 40 D4
Penleonard Cl *EXS* EX2 3 G5
Pennsylvania Cl *EXN* EX4 8 B5
Pennsylvania Crs *EXN* EX4 8 A5
Pennsylvania Pk *EXN* EX4 8 B4
Pennsylvania Rd *EXN* EX4 8 A5
Penny Cl *REXSW* EX6 26 A2
Perceval Rd *EXN* EX4 9 E3
Percy Rd *EXS* EX2 13 H5
Perriam's Pl *BUD* EX9 41 E4
Perridge Cl *EXS* EX2 12 D5
Perriman's Rw *EXM* EX8 * 38 A5
Perry Rd *EXN* EX4 7 H5
Perth Cl *EXN* EX4 8 C3
Peryam Crs *EXS* EX2 15 E4
Peterborough Rd *EXN* EX4 13 E1
Phear Av *EXM* EX8 38 B5
Philip Rd *EXN* EX4 8 D5
Phillipps Av *EXM* EX8 38 B3
Piazza Terracina *EXS* EX2 * 2 C6
Pier Head *EXM* EX8 43 G1
Pilton La *EX* EX1 9 H5
Pinbrook Rd *EXN* EX4 9 H4
Pinces Gdns *EXS* EX2 13 G5
Pinces Rd *EXS* EX2 13 G5
Pine Av *EXN* EX4 13 F1
Pineridge Cl *EXN* EX4 13 F4
Pines Rd *EXM* EX8 38 C1
The Pines *EXN* EX4 13 F1
Pine View Cl *EXM* EX8 39 F2
Pinhoe Rd *EXN* EX4 9 G5
Pinnbridge Ct *EX* EX1 * 10 A5
Pinncourt La *EX* EX1 10 B3
Pinn Hl *EX* EX1 10 B3
Pinn La *EX* EX1 10 A5
Pinn Valley Rd *EX* EX1 10 B4
Pinwood La *EXN* EX4 9 F3
Pinwood Meadow Dr *EXN* EX4 9 F3
Pippin Cl *EX* EX1 15 G2
Plassey Cl *EXN* EX4 8 B3
Playmoor Dr *EX* EX1 10 A4
Plumtree Dr *EXS* EX2 15 F4
Pocombe Br *REXSW* EX6 12 D5
Pocombe Hl *REXSW* EX6 12 D5
Point Ter *EXM* EX8 43 G1
Polehouse La *EXS* EX2 19 E2
Polsloe Rd *EX* EX1 3 H1
Poltimore Sq *EXN* EX4 2 D1
Poplar Cl *EXM* EX8 38 D1
EXS EX2 13 G5
The Poplars *EXN* EX4 10 A3
Porter's La *EXM* EX8 34 C1
Portland Av *EXM* EX8 44 B1
Portland St *EX* EX1 3 F2
Port Mer Cl *EXM* EX8 39 E1
Port Rd *DAW* EX7 42 A3
Post Office St *EX* EX1 2 D3
Pottles Cl *REXSW* EX6 26 A3
Pound Cl *TOP/EXT* EX3 22 A5
Pound La *EXM* EX8 38 B2
REXNE EX5 29 G2
TOP/EXT EX3 22 A5
Pound St *EXM* EX8 44 A1
Powderham Cl *TOP/EXT* EX3 22 A5
Powderham Crs *EXN* EX4 14 B1
Powderham Rd *EXS* EX2 13 F4
Powhay Mills *EXN* EX4 * 13 G3
Powlesland Rd *EXS* EX2 19 H2
Premier Pl *EXS* EX2 3 F5
Prescot Rd *EXN* EX4 13 E3
Preston St *EX* EX1 2 B4
Pretoria Rd *EX* EX1 3 H1
Priddis Cl *EXM* EX8 38 C1
Pridhams Wy *REXSW* EX6 26 A2
Priestley Av *EXN* EX4 9 F5
Primrose Lawn *EXN* EX4 6 D5
Prince Charles Cl *EXM* EX8 39 E3
Prince Charles Rd *EXN* EX4 8 C5
Prince of Wales Dr *EXM* EX8 39 E3
Prince of Wales Rd *EXN* EX4 7 H5
Princesshay *EX* EX1 2 C3
Prince's St West *EXS* EX2 13 G4
Prince's Sq *EXS* EX2 13 G5
Princes St *EXM* EX8 38 A5
Prince's St East *EXS* EX2 13 G5
Prince's St North *EXS* EX2 13 G4
Prince's St South *EXS* EX2 13 G5
Priory Gdns *EXN* EX4 * 2 A4
Priory Rd *EXN* EX4 8 C5
Prospect Gdns *EXN* EX4 14 C1
Prospect Pk *EXN* EX4 8 B5
Prospect Pl *EXN* EX4 13 G4
Puckridge Rd *EXN* EX4 9 H3
Pulling Rd *EXN* EX4 9 H3
Pulpit Wk *EXS* EX2 20 A4
Purcell Cl *EXS* EX2 15 G3
Pye Cnr *REXSW* EX6 24 D4
Pynes Hl *EXS* EX2 21 F1
Pytte Gdns *TOP/EXT* EX3 23 E4

Q

The Quadrangle *EXN* EX4 8 A5
The Quadrant *EXS* EX2 * 2 E5
The Quarries *EXN* EX4 12 D4
Quarry La *EXS* EX2 15 H4
Quarry Park Rd *EXS* EX2 15 G4
Quay Hl *EXS* EX2 2 B5
The Quay *EXS* EX2 2 C5
Queen's Crs *EXN* EX4 2 D1
Queen's Dr *EXM* EX8 44 C3
The Queen's Dr *EXN* EX4 7 H5
Queensland Dr *EXN* EX4 8 C3
Queen's Rd *BUD* EX9 40 D2
EXS EX2 13 G5
Queen's Ter *EXN* EX4 2 A1
Queen St *BUD* EX9 41 E4
EXM EX8 44 A1
EXN EX4 2 B2
Quintet Cl *EX* EX1 15 G3

R

Rackclose La *EXN* EX4 2 A4
Rack St *EX* EX1 2 B4
Raddenstile La *EXM* EX8 44 B1
Radford Rd *EXS* EX2 2 D5
Radnor Pl *EXS* EX2 2 E4
Ragg La *BUD* EX9 41 E4
Raglans *EXS* EX2 20 A3
Raleigh Rd *BUD* EX9 41 F3
EX EX1 3 F4
EXM EX8 44 A1
Rance Dr *EXM* EX8 39 E1
Raven Cl *EXN* EX4 8 A4
Rayners *REXSW* EX6 24 C5
Read Cl *EXM* EX8 38 C3
Rectory Dr *EXS* EX2 19 H3
Reddaway Dr *REXSW* EX6 25 H1
Redhills *BUD* EX9 41 E4
EXN EX4 12 D2
Redhills Cl *EXN* EX4 13 E2
Redlands Cl *EXN* EX4 9 E5
Red Lion La *EX* EX1 2 E1
Redvers Rd *EXN* EX4 13 G3
Redwood Cl *EXM* EX8 38 D1
Regency Crs *EXM* EX8 44 B1
Regents Ga *EXM* EX8 44 B1
Regent's Pk *EX* EX1 3 H2
Regent Sq *EX* EX1 3 K4
Regent St *EXS* EX2 13 G5
Rennes Dr *EXN* EX4 8 A4
Retail Park Cl *EXS* EX2 13 H5
The Retreat Dr *TOP/EXT* EX3 21 H5
Retreat Rd *TOP/EXT* EX3 27 E1
Rews Meadow *EX* EX1 10 A4
Rews Park Dr *EX* EX1 10 B4
Rexona Cl *EXS* EX2 19 G1
Reynolds Cl *EXN* EX4 9 H4
Ribston Av *EX* EX1 15 G2
Rices Ms *EXS* EX2 13 G5
Richards Cl *EXM* EX8 38 D2
Richmond Rd *EXM* EX8 38 D4
EXN EX4 2 A2
Ridgeway *EXN* EX4 7 G2
Ridge Wy *REXSW* EX6 36 A2
The Ridings *TOP/EXT* EX3 28 A2
Rifford Rd *EXS* EX2 15 F4
Rill La *BUD* EX9 41 F4
Ringswell Av *EX* EX1 15 G2
River Front *TOP/EXT* EX3 27 H4
Rivermead Av *EXM* EX8 38 A2
River Mdw *EXS* EX2 14 A5
Rivermead Rd *EXS* EX2 14 B5
Riverside Rd *TOP/EXT* EX3 21 H5
Rivers Wk *TOP/EXT* EX3 21 G4
Riverview Dr *EXN* EX4 7 F5
River View Ter *REXSW* EX6 26 B3
Roberts Rd *EXS* EX2 2 D5
Roche Gdn *EXS* EX2 21 E3
Rodney Cl *EXM* EX8 39 G5
Rolle Rd *BUD* EX9 41 E4
EXM EX8 44 B2
Rollestone Crs *EXN* EX4 8 C3
Rolle St *EXM* EX8 44 A1
Rolle Vls *EXM* EX8 44 A1
Romsey Dr *EXS* EX2 3 G5
Ropewalk House *EXM* EX8 * 43 G1
Rosebank Crs *EXN* EX4 8 B4
Rosebarn Av *EXN* EX4 8 B4
Rosebarn La *EXN* EX4 8 B3
Rosebery Rd *EXM* EX8 38 A5
EXN EX4 8 C5
Roseland Av *EX* EX1 15 E2
Roseland Crs *EX* EX1 15 E2
Roseland Dr *EX* EX1 3 K4
Rosemary St *EXN* EX4 13 F3
Rosemont Ct *EXS* EX2 19 H2
The Rosemullion *BUD* EX9 * 41 E4
Roseway *EXM* EX8 39 E4
Rosewood Crs *REXNE* EX5 23 F1
Rosewood Ter *EXN* EX4 8 B5
Ross Cl *EX* EX1 10 B4
Rougemont Ct *REXSW* EX6 * 25 H2
Roundhill Cl *EXN* EX4 7 G2
Roundhouse La *EXM* EX8 38 B2
Roundtable Meet *EXN* EX4 9 F4
Rowan Wy *EXN* EX4 13 F1
Rowlstone Cl *EXM* EX8 38 C1
The Royal Av *EXM* EX8 37 H5
Royal Cl *EXS* EX2 19 H4
Royal Crs *EXS* EX2 15 H5
Royal Wy *REXSW* EX6 36 D4
Rugby Rd *EXN* EX4 13 G4
Rushforth Pl *EXN* EX4 7 E5
Russell St *EX* EX1 3 F2
Russell Ter *EXN* EX4 * 2 A1
Russell Wy *EXS* EX2 15 G5
Russet Av *EX* EX1 15 G2
Rutherford St *EXS* EX2 15 E4
Rydon La *EXS* EX2 21 G1
REXNE EX5 29 E4
TOP/EXT EX3 28 B4
Rydon Pk *EXS* EX2 * 15 H4
Ryll Cl *EXM* EX8 38 A5
Ryll Court Dr *EXM* EX8 38 B5
Ryll Gv *EXM* EX8 38 B5

S

Sadler Cl *EXM* EX8 39 E4
Sailmakers Ct *EXM* EX8 * 43 G1
St Andrew's Cl *REXSW* EX6 31 E2
St Andrew's Rd *EXM* EX8 43 H1
EXN EX4 7 F4
St Anne's Rd *EX* EX1 14 C1
St Bernard's Cl *EXS* EX2 2 E7
St Briac Wy *EXM* EX8 39 E1
St Davids *EXN* EX4 * 13 G1
St David's Hl *EXN* EX4 13 G1
St Davids Pl *EXN* EX4 * 13 G1
St Davids Ter *EXN* EX4 * 2 A2
St German's Rd *EXN* EX4 8 A5
St Hill Cl *EXS* EX2 19 G1
St Ida's Cl *EXS* EX2 18 D2
St James Cl *EXN* EX4 14 B1
St James' Rd *EXN* EX4 14 B1
St James Ter *EXN* EX4 * 14 B1
St John's Rd *EXM* EX8 39 E3
EXN EX4 14 C1
St Katherines Rd *EXN* EX4 9 E5
St Lawrence Crs *EX* EX1 15 G2
St Leonard's Av *EXS* EX2 2 D6
St Leonard's Pl *EXS* EX2 2 E5
St Leonard's Rd *EXS* EX2 2 E5
St Loyes Rd *EXS* EX2 15 E3
St Loye's Ter *EXS* EX2 15 E4
St Malo Cl *EXM* EX8 39 E1
St Margarets Ter
TOP/EXT EX3 * 27 F1
St Margaret's Vw *EXM* EX8 39 G5
St Marks Av *EXN* EX4 14 D1
St Mary Steps Ter *EX* EX1 * 2 B4
St Mathews Wk *EX* EX1 * 3 F2
St Matthews Cl *EX* EX1 3 G2
St Michael's Cl *EXS* EX2 19 H3
REXNE EX5 11 F5
St Michael's Hl *REXNE* EX5 11 F5
St Olave's Cl *EXN* EX4 2 B4
St Peters Mt *EXN* EX4 12 D2
St Petrocks Cl *EXS* EX2 3 F5
St Sevan Wy *EXM* EX8 39 E1
St Sidwell's Av *EXN* EX4 14 B1
St Thomas Ct *EXS* EX2 13 G4
Salem Pl *EX* EX1 * 3 F1
Salisbury Rd *EXM* EX8 38 A5
EXN EX4 8 C5
Salmonpool La *EXS* EX2 14 C5
Salter's Rd *EXS* EX2 15 F3
Salterton Ct *EXM* EX8 39 F4
Salterton Rd *EXM* EX8 39 H3
EXM EX8 44 B1
Salting Hl *BUD* EX9 41 G4
Salutary Mt *EXS* EX2 * 3 J4
Sampson's Hl *EXS* EX2 24 B2
Sampsons La *EX* EX1 3 H1
Sanders Rd *EXN* EX4 10 A4
Sandfords *REXSW* EX6 30 C1
Sandford Wk *EX* EX1 3 F2
Sandpiper Dr *TOP/EXT* EX3 28 A4
Sannerville Wy *EXS* EX2 20 C4
REXSW EX6 21 E5
Sargent Cl *EX* EX1 15 G2
Sarlsdown Rd *EXM* EX8 38 C5
Savile Rd *EXN* EX4 13 F3
Savoy Hl *EXN* EX4 9 E3
Saxon Av *EXN* EX4 10 A3
Saxon Rd *EX* EX1 3 K3
School Hl *EXM* EX8 34 C4
REXSW EX6 42 D1
School La *EXM* EX8 38 B3
EXS EX2 21 E2
School Rd *EXS* EX2 13 G4
Scott Av *EXS* EX2 14 D5
Scott Dr *EXM* EX8 38 B2
Scratch Face La *REXSW* EX6 18 C1
Seabrook Av *EXS* EX2 21 G4
Seafield Av *EXM* EX8 38 A2
Second Av *EX* EX1 3 J2
TOP/EXT EX3 21 G4
Sedgeclaire Cl *EX* EX1 10 B4
Senate Wy *EXM* EX8 38 D3
Sentrys Orch *REXSW* EX6 26 B3
Sercombes Gdns *REXSW* EX6 36 C4
Seymore Cl *EXM* EX8 38 B2
Seymour Ct *EXM* EX8 38 B2
Seymour Rd *EXM* EX8 38 B2
Shackleton Cl *EXM* EX8 38 B2
Shaftesbury Rd *EXS* EX2 13 G4
Shakespeare Rd *EXS* EX2 14 D5
Shakespeare Wy *EXM* EX8 35 G5
Shelley Cl *EXS* EX2 19 G1
Shelly Reach *EXM* EX8 43 H1
Shelly Rd *EXM* EX8 43 G1
Shelton Pl *EX* EX1 * 3 K3
Shepherd's Hl *EXS* EX2 20 D2
Sheppard Rd *EXN* EX4 8 B3
Sheppard's Rw *EXM* EX8 38 A5
Sherbrook Cl *BUD* EX9 40 C4
Sherbrook Hl *BUD* EX9 40 D4
Shercroft Cl *REXNE* EX5 11 G3
Sheridan Rd *EXN* EX4 9 G5
Sherwell Cl *DAW* EX7 42 C5
Sherwood Cl *EXS* EX2 3 J5
Sherwood Dr *EXM* EX8 38 D1
Shillingford La *REXSW* EX6 24 C2
Shillingford Rd *EXS* EX2 19 G4
Ship La *REXNE* EX5 11 F5
Shirley Cl *EXM* EX8 35 H5
Shooting Marsh Stile *EXS* EX2 2 B6
Shortwood Cl *BUD* EX9 40 D2
Shute Meadow St *EXM* EX8 * 38 A5
Shutterton Br *DAW* EX7 42 B5
Shutterton La *DAW* EX7 42 B5
Sidmouth Rd *EXS* EX2 15 H4
EXS EX2 16 B4
Sidwell St *EX* EX1 2 D2
Sigford Rd *EXS* EX2 20 B3
Silver Birch Cl *EXS* EX2 15 E5
Silverdale *EXM* EX8 39 E1
Silver La *EX* EX1 3 F1
The Silvers *EXS* EX2 * 22 B1
Silver Ter *EXN* EX4 * 2 A2
Silverton Rd *EXS* EX2 20 B3
Simey Cl *EXN* EX4 13 F1
Sivell Ms *EXS* EX2 * 3 K4
Sivell Pl *EXS* EX2 3 K4
Slittercombe La *REXSW* EX6 32 D5
Smith Field Rd *EXS* EX2 19 G3
Smiths Ct *EXS* EX2 2 B7
Smythen St *EX* EX1 2 B4
Solar Crs *EXN* EX4 13 E4
Somerset Av *EXN* EX4 13 E4
Somerville Cl *EXM* EX8 38 D3
South Av *EX* EX1 3 H2
Southbrook Rd *EXS* EX2 21 E2
Southernhay East *EX* EX1 2 C4
Southernhay Gdns *EX* EX1 2 D3
Southernhay West *EX* EX1 2 D2
Southern Rd *EXM* EX8 38 A4
Southern Wd *EXM* EX8 39 E2
South Farm Rd *BUD* EX9 41 G1
South Ga *EXS* EX2 2 C5
South Lawn Ter *EX* EX1 3 K3
South Pde *BUD* EX9 41 F4
Southport Av *EXN* EX4 13 E3
South St *EX* EX1 2 B4
EXM EX8 44 A1
South View Ter *EXN* EX4 8 B5
South West Coast Pth
BUD EX9 40 D4
EXM EX8 44 D3
REXSW EX6 27 E3
Sovereign Cl *EXM* EX8 39 E3
Sowden La *EXM* EX8 34 C5
Sowton La *REXNE* EX5 16 C2
Spencer Cl *EXM* EX8 39 E2
Spenser Av *EXS* EX2 14 D5
Spicer Rd *EX* EX1 3 F4
Spider's La *EXM* EX8 38 C1
Spinney Cl *EXS* EX2 15 G4
Spinning Pth *EXN* EX4 * 14 B1
Springfield Rd *EXM* EX8 38 B3
EXN EX4 8 B5
Spruce Cl *EXM* EX8 38 D1
EXN EX4 9 F3
The Square *EXN* EX4 * 7 F5
Staddon Cl *EX* EX1 15 F1
Stadium Wy *EXN* EX4 14 B1
Staffick Cl *REXSW* EX6 36 A1
Stafford Rd *EXN* EX4 13 F3
Stanford Rd *EXS* EX2 15 G3
Stanley Ms *BUD* EX9 * 41 E3
Stanley Sq *TOP/EXT* EX3 * 27 F2
Stanley Wk *EXM* EX8 35 H5
Stanwey *EX* EX1 15 E3
Staplake La *REXSW* EX6 36 C5
Staplake Ri *REXSW* EX6 36 C3
Staplake Rd *REXSW* EX6 36 C3
Star Barton La *REXNE* EX5 6 C1

Station Rd *BUD* EX9 41 E3
EX EX1 10 A4
EXN EX4 7 F5
EXS EX2 18 D2
REXSW EX6 27 E3
TOP/EXT EX3 27 F1
TOP/EXT EX3 28 A5
Station Yd *EXN* EX4 2 A2
Steeple Dr *EXS* EX2 19 H4
Stepcote Hl *EX* EX1 * 2 A4
Steps Cl *EX* EX1 10 A4
Stevenstone Rd *EXM* EX8 38 D5
Stewart Cl *EXM* EX8 39 E3
Stocker Rd *EXN* EX4 7 H4
Stoke Hl *EXN* EX4 8 C5
Stoke Hill Crs *EXN* EX4 8 C4
Stoke Lyne *EXM* EX8 38 C3
Stoke Meadow Cl *EXN* EX4 8 C3
Stoke Rd *EXN* EX4 7 G1
Stokes Md *REXNE* EX5 29 G3
Stoke Valley Rd *EXN* EX4 8 B2
Stoneborough La *BUD* EX9 41 F3
Stone La *EXM* EX8 34 C4
Stoneyford Pk *BUD* EX9 41 F3
Stony La *EXM* EX8 34 D1
Stover Ct *EX* EX1 2 E1
Strand *TOP/EXT* EX3 27 F2
The Strand *EXM* EX8 34 B4
EXM EX8 44 A1
REXSW EX6 36 D3
Strand Vw *TOP/EXT* EX3 27 F2
Stratford Av *EXN* EX4 9 G5
Strawberry Av *EXS* EX2 20 A3
Strawberry Hl *EXM* EX8 34 D4
Stream Ct *EXS* EX2 2 B6
Streatham Dr *EXN* EX4 7 G5
Streatham Ri *EXN* EX4 7 G5
Stuart Rd *EX* EX1 3 K3
Sturges Rd *EXM* EX8 38 D4
Sullivan Rd *EXS* EX2 15 G3
Summer Cl *EXM* EX8 39 E4
EXN EX4 9 F5
Summerfield *REXNE* EX5 29 G2
Summerland St *EX* EX1 2 E1
Summer La *EXM* EX8 38 A1
EXN EX4 9 F4
Summerway *EXN* EX4 9 G5
Sunhill Av *TOP/EXT* EX3 22 B5
Sunnymoor Cl *EX* EX1 10 B4
Sunwine Pl *EXM* EX8 44 B1
Surbiton Crs *EXN* EX4 13 F4
Sussex Cl *EXN* EX4 13 E4
Swains Ct *TOP/EXT* EX3 * 27 E1
Swains Rd *BUD* EX9 41 F3
Swallowfield Rd *EXS* EX2 21 E1
Swan Rd *REXSW* EX6 36 C4
Swan Yd *EXN* EX4 13 G3
Sweetbrier La *EX* EX1 15 F3
Swiss Cl *EXM* EX8 38 B1
Sycamore Av *DAW* EX7 42 C5
Sycamore Cl *EX* EX1 15 F3
EXM EX8 39 F2
Sydney Pl *EXS* EX2 * 2 A6
Sydney Rd *EXS* EX2 13 G4
Sylvan Av *EXN* EX4 8 B4
Sylvan Cl *EXM* EX8 38 A2
Sylvania Dr *EXN* EX4 8 C3
Sylvan Rd *EXN* EX4 8 B4
Synagogue Pl *EXN* EX4 2 B3

T

Taddiford Rd *EXN* EX4 7 G5
Taddyforde Ct *EXN* EX4 * 7 G5
Taddyforde Est *EXN* EX4 * 7 G5
Tamarisk Cl *EXN* EX4 9 F3
Tan La *EXS* EX2 2 B7
Tappers Cl *TOP/EXT* EX3 27 F1
Taps Cl *REXSW* EX6 26 B2
Tarbet Av *EX* EX1 14 D1
Taunton Cl *EXS* EX2 19 G1
Tavistock Rd *EXN* EX4 13 G1
Tedburn Rd *EXN* EX4 12 B3
Tedstone La *EXM* EX8 35 E4
Telegraph Hl *REXSW* EX6 30 C5
Telford Rd *EXN* EX4 13 G1
Temple Rd *EXS* EX2 2 D5
Tennyson Av *EXS* EX2 14 D5
Tennyson Wy *EXM* EX8 35 G5
Thackeray Rd *EXN* EX4 9 G5
Third Av *EX* EX1 3 J2
TOP/EXT EX3 21 H4
Thomas Cl *EXM* EX8 35 G5
Thomas La *EXN* EX4 * 7 G5
Thompson Rd *EX* EX1 15 E1
Thornberry Av *EX* EX1 15 F2
Thorn Cl *EX* EX1 15 F2
Thornfield Cl *EXM* EX8 38 A2
Thornpark Ri *EX* EX1 15 F2
Thornton Hl *EXN* EX4 8 A5
Thorpe Av *EXM* EX8 38 B1
Three Corner Pl *EXS* EX2 20 A3
Thurlow Rd *EXN* EX4 8 C5
Tidwell Cl *BUD* EX9 41 E2
Tidwell Rd *BUD* EX9 41 E2
Tintagel Cl *EXN* EX4 8 D3
Tithebarn Copse *EX* EX1 10 B5
Tithebarn La *EX* EX1 10 B5
Toby La *REXNE* EX5 29 H1
Tollards Rd *EXS* EX2 21 E2
Topsham Rd *EXS* EX2 2 E6
Tor Cl *EXN* EX4 9 E4
Toronto Rd *EXN* EX4 14 B1
Tottons Ct *EXS* EX2 19 G3
Towerfield *TOP/EXT* EX3 22 A4
Tower St *EXM* EX8 44 A1
Tower Wk *EXS* EX2 20 A3
Townfield *REXSW* EX6 26 A2
Town La *REXNE* EX5 29 G3
Trafalgar Rd *EXM* EX8 34 C3
Travershes Cl *EXM* EX8 38 B3
Trefusis Pl *EXM* EX8 44 A2
Trefusis Ter *EXM* EX8 44 A2
Trentbridge Sq *EXS* EX2 15 G4
Tresillian Gdns *TOP/EXT* EX3 27 F2
Tresillian Gdns *EXN* EX4 8 C5
Trews Weir Ct *EXS* EX2 2 E7
Trews Weir Reach *EXS* EX2 2 E7
Trinfield Av *EXM* EX8 38 B3
Trinity Rd *EXM* EX8 43 G1
Tristan Cl *EXN* EX4 9 E3
Trood La *EXS* EX2 20 B5
Truro Dr *EXM* EX8 35 H5
EXN EX4 13 E1
Trusham Rd *EXS* EX2 14 A5
Tuckfield Cl *EXS* EX2 15 E4
Tudor Ct *EXN* EX4 2 A4
Tudor St *EXN* EX4 2 A4
Tugela Ter *REXNE* EX5 * 16 C5
Turner Av *EXM* EX8 38 C5
Twinaway La *EXS* EX2 18 C4
Twoacre Ct *EXS* EX2 19 G3
Two Stone La *REXSW* EX6 30 A1

U

Underhill Crs *EXM* EX8 34 C5
Underhill Ter *TOP/EXT* EX3 27 F1
Union Rd *EXN* EX4 8 B5
Union St *EXM* EX8 44 A1
EXS EX2 13 G4
Uplands Dr *EXN* EX4 8 D4
Upper Church St *EXM* EX8 44 A1
Upper Paul St *EXN* EX4 2 B2
Upper Stoneborough La
BUD EX9 41 E3
Upper West Ter *BUD* EX9 41 E3
Upton Pyne Hl *REXNE* EX5 7 F1

V

Vachell Crs *EXS* EX2 15 H3
Vale Rd *EXM* EX8 38 D5
Vales Rd *BUD* EX9 41 F3
Valley Rd *EXN* EX4 13 F1
REXNE EX5 17 F5
Valley Wy *EXM* EX8 39 E1
Vansittart Dr *EXM* EX8 38 C1
Varco Sq *EXS* EX2 15 G4
Vaughan Ri *EX* EX1 15 F2
Vaughan Rd *EX* EX1 15 F2
Veitch Gdns *EXS* EX2 19 H4
Velwell Rd *EXN* EX4 13 H1
Venny Br *EXN* EX4 9 H4
Verney St *EX* EX1 2 E1
Vernon Rd *EXM* EX8 38 D2
Vestry Dr *EXS* EX2 19 H3
Vicarage Gdns *EXS* EX2 * 13 G4
Vicarage La *EXN* EX4 10 A3
Vicarage Rd *REXSW* EX6 42 D1
Victoria Park Rd *EXS* EX2 3 G5
Victoria Pl *BUD* EX9 41 E4
EXM EX8 44 A1
Victoria Rd *EXM* EX8 43 H1
EXN EX4 8 B5
TOP/EXT EX3 27 F1
Victoria St *EXN* EX4 8 B5
Victoria Wy *EXM* EX8 43 H1
Victor La *EX* EX1 15 E3
Victor St *EX* EX1 15 E3
Village Cl *EXM* EX8 39 F5
Vine Cl *EXS* EX2 2 E5
Vision Hill Rd *BUD* EX9 41 F2
Vuefield Hl *EXS* EX2 13 E5
Vyvyan Ct *EX* EX1 * 15 E3

W

Wade Cl *EXM* EX8 39 E4
Waggoners Wy *EXN* EX4 7 G5
Wallace Av *EXN* EX4 9 F5
Walls Cl *EXM* EX8 38 D2
Walnut Cl *REXSW* EX6 26 A2
Walnut Gv *EXM* EX8 38 C5
Walnut Rd *EXS* EX2 20 D1
Walpole Cl *EXN* EX4 9 G4
Walton Rd *EXS* EX2 15 G3
Warborough Hl *REXSW* EX6 36 A2
Wardrew Rd *EXN* EX4 13 F3
Waring Bowen Ct *EXS* EX2 * 20 D2
Warneford Gdns *EXM* EX8 39 E2
Warren Dr *BUD* EX9 41 F2
Warren La *EXN* EX4 2 D1
Warwick Av *EX* EX1 15 G3
Warwick Rd *EX* EX1 15 G2
Warwick Wy *EXN* EX4 9 G5
Waterbeer St *EXN* EX4 * 2 B3
Water Ga *EXS* EX2 2 C5
Water La *EXS* EX2 2 B6
Waterloo Rd *EXS* EX2 13 G5
Waterside *EXS* EX2 * 2 C6
Waterslade La *REXNE* EX5 11 F5
Watery La *REXNE* EX5 29 F2
Waverley Av *EXN* EX4 14 A1
Waverley Rd *EXM* EX8 38 A4
Waybrook Crs *EXS* EX2 20 A3
Waybrook La *EXS* EX2 19 G5
Wayland Av *EXS* EX2 3 F6
Wayside Crs *EX* EX1 15 F1
Wear Barton Rd *EXS* EX2 21 F3
Wear Cl *EXS* EX2 21 G4
Webley Rd *EXS* EX2 13 F5
Weirfield Rd *EXS* EX2 2 D7
Welcome St *EXS* EX2 2 B7
Wellington Rd *EXS* EX2 13 G5
Well Oak Pk *EXS* EX2 14 D5
Wellpark Cl *EXN* EX4 13 F3
Well St *EXN* EX4 2 E1
REXSW EX6 36 D4
Wellswood Gdns *EXN* EX4 13 E4
Wendover Wy *EXS* EX2 21 F1
Wentworth Gdns *EXN* EX4 13 E4
Wesley Wy *EXS* EX2 19 H3
Wessex Cl *TOP/EXT* EX3 21 H5
Wessex Est *EXN* EX4 * 13 G1
West Av *EXN* EX4 8 A5
Westbourne Ter *BUD* EX9 40 D4
Westbrook Cl *EXN* EX4 9 F5
Westcombe *EXS* EX2 19 H3
West Down La *EXM* EX8 39 F5
West Down Vw *EXM* EX8 45 H2
Western Dr *REXSW* EX6 36 D4
Western Rd *EXN* EX4 13 G3
Western Wy *EX* EX1 2 E2
EXS EX2 2 B5
Westfield Cl *BUD* EX9 41 E3
Westfield Rd *BUD* EX9 41 E3
West Field Rd *REXSW* EX6 26 B3
West Garth Ct *EXN* EX4 * 7 F3
West Garth Rd *EXN* EX4 7 G3
West Grove Rd *EXS* EX2 2 E5
West Hl *BUD* EX9 40 D4
West Hill Gdns *BUD* EX9 * 40 D4
West Hill La *BUD* EX9 40 D3
Westminster Cl *EXM* EX8 38 D1
Westminster Rd *EXN* EX4 13 E2
Westown Rd *EXS* EX2 18 C2
West St *EX* EX1 2 A4
West Ter *BUD* EX9 41 E3
EX EX1 3 K3
West View Ter *EXN* EX4 * 2 A4
Westward Dr *EXM* EX8 38 B5
Westwood Hl *REXSW* EX6 42 C1
Westwood La *REXSW* EX6 12 B4
Weycroft Cl *EX* EX1 15 H2
Wheatley Cl *EXN* EX4 13 E3
Wheatsheaf Wy *EXS* EX2 19 G2
Whiddon La *EXS* EX2 18 B3
Whipton Barton Rd *EX* EX1 15 F1
Whipton La *EX* EX1 15 F2
Whipton Rd *EXN* EX4 9 E5
Whipton Village Rd *EXN* EX4 9 F5
Whitchurch Av *EXS* EX2 15 F4
Whitebeam Cl *EXN* EX4 9 F3
Whitehall La *TOP/EXT* EX3 22 A3
Whiteside Cl *EXS* EX2 15 G4
White St *TOP/EXT* EX3 27 F2
Whitethorn Pk *EXN* EX4 8 A2
Whiteway Dr *EX* EX1 15 E2
Whitman Cl *EXM* EX8 35 G5
Whitycombe Wy *EXN* EX4 6 D5
Widecombe Wy *EXN* EX4 8 C3
Widgery Rd *EXN* EX4 9 E5
Wilcocks Rd *EXN* EX4 9 H4
Wilford Rd *EXS* EX2 15 F3
Willeys Av *EXS* EX2 2 A7
Willeys Ct *EXS* EX2 2 B7
Williams Av *EXS* EX2
Willmott Cl *EXM* EX8 3
Willoughby Cl *EXM* EX8 3
Willow Av *EXM* EX8 3
Willow Ct *EXS* EX2 1
The Willows *EXS* EX2 2
Willow Wk *EXN* EX4
Willow Wy *DAW* EX7 4
Willsdown Rd *EXS* EX2 1
Wilton Wy *EX* EX1 1
Wiltshire Cl *EXN* EX4 1
Winchester Av *EXN* EX4 1
Winchester Dr *EXM* EX8 3
Windermere Cl *EXN* EX4 1
Windsor Cl *EXN* EX4 1
Windsor Dr *DAW* EX7 4
Windsor Sq *EXM* EX8 3
Winslade Park Av *REXNE* EX5 2
Winston Rd *EXM* EX8 3
Withycombe Park Dr *EXM* EX8 3
Withycombe Rd *EXM* EX8 3
Withycombe Village Rd
EXM EX8 3
Wonford Rd *EXS* EX2
Wonford St *EXS* EX2 1
Woodah Rd *EXN* EX4 1
Woodbine Ter *EXN* EX4
Woodbury Rd *REXNE* EX5 2
TOP/EXT EX3 2
Woodbury Vw *EXS* EX2 1
Woodfield Cl *EXM* EX8 3
Woodland Rd *EX* EX1 1
Woodlands *BUD* EX9 4
Woodlands Dr *EXM* EX8 3
Woodlands Wy *REXNE* EX5 1
Wood La *EXM* EX8 3
Woodleigh Cl *EXN* EX4
Woodstock Rd *EXS* EX2 1
Woodville Rd *EXM* EX8 3
EXS EX2 1
Woodwater La *EXS* EX2 1
Woolsery Av *EXN* EX4
Woolsery Cl *EXN* EX4
Woolsery Gv *EXN* EX4
Worcester Ms *EXN* EX4 * 1
Wordsworth Cl *EXM* EX8 3
Wotton La *EXM* EX8 3
Wreford's Cl *EXN* EX4
Wreford's Dr *EXN* EX4
Wreford's La *EXN* EX4
Wreford's Link *EXN* EX4
Wrentham Est *EXN* EX4 *
Wykes Rd *EX* EX1 1
Wynards *EX* EX1 *
Wyndham Av *EX* EX1
Wynford Rd *EXN* EX4

Y

Yeoford Wy *EXS* EX2 2
Yew Tree Cl *EXM* EX8 3
EXN EX4
York Cl *EXM* EX8 3
York Rd *EXN* EX4
York Ter *EXN* EX4 * 1

Index - featured places

A La Ronde (NT) *EXM* EX8 38 A1
Alphington Combined School *EXS* EX2 19 H2
Alphington Sports Club *EXS* EX2 19 H2
Annexe London Hospital *EXN* EX4 8 A5
Ashton Business Centre *EXS* EX2 19 H1
Atkinson Unit *EXN* EX4 9 E5
Axehayes Farm Caravan Site *REXNE* EX5 17 H5
Barley Lane Special School *EXN* EX4 12 D4
Barnfield Theatre *EX* EX1 2 D3
Barn Hotel *EXM* EX8 44 C2
Barton Cross Hotel *REXNE* EX5 4 B2
Bassetts Farm Primary School *EXM* EX8 39 E3
The Beacon CE VA Primary School *EXM* EX8 43 H1
Bishops Court Industrial Estate *EXS* EX2 16 A5
Bonhay Business Centre *EXN* EX4 13 G3
Bradley Rowe F & M School *EXS* EX2 14 D5
Brixington Community Primary School *EXM* EX8 38 C2
Buckerell Lodge Hotel *EXS* EX2 14 C5
Budleigh Salterton FC *BUD* EX9 40 D2
Budleigh Salterton Hospital *BUD* EX9 41 F3
Cavendish Hotel *EXM* EX8 43 H1
Central CE First School *EXS* EX2 2 E6
Central CE Middle School *EXS* EX2 2 E6
City Industrial Estate *EXS* EX2 2 C7
Clifton Hill Sports Centre, Golf Range & Ski Slope *EX* EX1 3 G1
Clyst Honiton School *REXNE* EX5 17 F1
Clyst St George Lady Seawards CE Primary School *TOP/EXT* EX3 23 E5
Clyst St Mary Primary School *REXNE* EX5 16 C5
Cockwood Primary School *REXSW* EX6 42 D1
Cofton Country Holiday Park *REXSW* EX6 42 B2
Countess Weir Combined School *EXS* EX2 21 F3
County Ground Stadium *EXS* EX2 13 G4
Cowick First School *EXN* EX4 13 F4
Cowley Bridge Road Business Park *EXN* EX4 7 F4
Cygnet New Theatre *EXS* EX2 2 C5
Darts Farm *TOP/EXT* EX3 27 H1
Dawlish Warren National Nature Reserve *DAW* EX7 43 E4
Devon Cliffs Holiday Park *EXM* EX8 45 G1
Devon & Exeter Squash Club *EXN* EX4 8 A5
Devon Hotel *EXS* EX2 20 B4
Devon Record Office *EXS* EX2 16 A2
Dinan Way Trading Estate *EXM* EX8 39 F3
The Dolphin School *EXM* EX8 44 B1
Dunns Business Centre *EXS* EX2 20 A1
East Devon Golf Club *BUD* EX9 40 C4
Ellen Tinkham Special School *EX* EX1 16 A1
Elm Grove School *TOP/EXT* EX3 27 F1
Emmanuel School *EXN* EX4 14 B1
Exe Estuary RSPB Reserve *REXSW* EX6 26 D3
Exe Sailing Club *EXM* EX8 43 G1
The Exeter Academy *EXN* EX4 8 B4
Exeter Airport *REXNE* EX5 11 H5
Exeter Business School *EXN* EX4 2 D2
Exeter Cathedral School *EX* EX1 2 C4
Exeter CC *EXN* EX4 8 A5
Exeter Cemetery *EX* EX1 3 K1
Exeter City FC *EXN* EX4 14 B1
Exeter College *EXN* EX4 2 A2
EXS EX2 20 A1
Exeter College (Episcopal Centre) *EXN* EX4 2 A3
Exeter College (International Centre) *EXN* EX4 13 G1
Exeter & Devon Crematorium *EXS* EX2 20 D1
Exeter Golf & Country Club *EXS* EX2 21 G3
Exeter Junior School *EXS* EX2 3 H4
The Exeter Nuffield Hospital *EXS* EX2 3 H6
Exeter Phoenix Arts Centre *EXN* EX4 2 B2
The Exeter Picture House *EXN* EX4 2 A4
Exeter Race Course *REXSW* EX6 30 A5
Exeter RFC & Speedway *EXN* EX4 13 G4
Exeter Road Primary School *EXM* EX8 38 A5
Exeter St Thomas CC *EXS* EX2 19 H1
Exeter School *EXS* EX2 3 H5
Exeter Technical College *EX* EX1 2 B4
Exminster Primary School *REXSW* EX6 26 A2
Exmouth Community College *EXM* EX8 38 B4
Exmouth CC *EXM* EX8 44 B2
Exmouth Hospital *EXM* EX8 38 B5
Exmouth Indoor Market *EXM* EX8 38 A5
Exmouth Leisure Centre *EXM* EX8 4
Exmouth RFC *EXM* EX8 3
Exmouth Town FC *EXM* EX8 3
Exwick Middle School *EXN* EX4 1
Fairlynch Museum *BUD* EX9 4
Foxhayes First School *EXN* EX4 1
Gipsy Hill Country House Hotel *EX* EX1 1
Golden Sands Holiday Park *DAW* EX7 4
Guildhall Shopping Centre *EXN* EX4
Harlequins Shopping Centre *EXN* EX4
Haven Banks Sailing & Canoeing Club *EXS* EX2
Heavitree Health Centre *EX* EX1
Hill Barton Business Park *REXNE* EX5 2
HM Prison *EXN* EX4
Honeylands Hospital for Children *EXN* EX4
Hope House Montessori School *TOP/EXT* EX3 2
Hotel Barcelona *EXS* EX2
Hylton Pre Preparatory School *EXS* EX2
Ide First School *EXS* EX2 1

eper's Lodge *P/EXT* EX3 ..... 27 H1
Stocker Middle School *N* EX4 ..... 13 F4
CE Primary School *KSW* EX6 ..... 24 D5
ford International ravan Park *XSW* EX6 ..... 30 C1
el Business Park *S* EX2 ..... 21 H2
mith First School EX1 ..... 3 H1
mith Middle School EX1 ..... 3 H1
don Hospital *W* EX7 ..... 42 A4
Bridge Business Park *XNE* EX5 ..... 23 F2
nam CE Primary School *M* EX8 ..... 39 F5
on Business Park *M* EX8 ..... 39 F3
e Trading Estate *XNE* EX5 ..... 11 G2
brook Complementary alth Centre *N* EX4 ..... 2 D1
stone CE Primary School *M* EX8 ..... 34 C4
alen Court School *S* EX2 ..... 3 G5
r Hotel *M* EX8 ..... 44 A1
tree *S* EX2 ..... 24 A1
ool Primary School *M* EX8 ..... 38 C4
n Barton Trading Estate *S* EX2 ..... 13 H5
S EX2 ..... 20 A2
laynard School EX1 ..... 3 F3
ow House Clinic *N* EX4 ..... 13 H1
bowl *S* EX2 ..... 2 C6
Coffee House EX1 ..... 2 C3
gomery Combined hool *EXN* EX4 ..... 13 F3
t Pleasant Health Centre *N* EX4 ..... 8 C5
The New School *REXSW* EX6 ..... 26 A2
Newtown First School *EX* EX1 ..... 3 F2
Northcott Theatre *EXN* EX4 ..... 7 H4
Northernhay Gate *EXN* EX4 ..... 2 B2
Nutwell Court *EXM* EX8 ..... 34 B2
Odeon Cinema *EXN* EX4 ..... 2 E1
Old Tudor House *EXN* EX4 ..... 13 G3
Park Five Business Centre *EXS* EX2 ..... 16 A4
Peppermint Park *DAW* EX7 ..... 42 D5
Pinbrook Industrial Estate *EXN* EX4 ..... 9 H4
Pinhoe CE Combined School *EXN* EX4 ..... 10 A4
Pooh Cottage Holiday Park *BUD* EX9 ..... 40 B1
Post Graduate Medical School *EXS* EX2 ..... 3 J5
Pound Lane Trading Estate *EXM* EX8 ..... 38 C3
Powderham Castle *REXSW* EX6 ..... 33 F5
Premier Travel Inn *EXS* EX2 ..... 21 E2
The Priory High School *EXS* EX2 ..... 20 C1
Pyramids Swimming & Leisure Centre *EX* EX1 ..... 2 E3
Quay House Visitor Centre *EXS* EX2 ..... 2 B5
Queen's Court Hotel *EXN* EX4 ..... 2 A1
Redhills Combined School *EXN* EX4 ..... 13 F3
Riverside Leisure Centre *EXS* EX2 ..... 2 A6
Rolle Clinic *EXM* EX8 ..... 44 A1
Rougemont Castle *EXN* EX4 ..... 2 C1
Royal Albert Memorial Museum *EXN* EX4 ..... 2 B2
Royal Beacon Hotel *EXM* EX8 ..... 44 A1
Royal Clarence Hotel *EX* EX1 ..... 2 C3
Royal Devon & Exeter Hospital (Heavitree) *EX* EX1 ..... 3 G3
Royal Devon & Exeter Hospital (Wonford) *EXS* EX2 ..... 3 J6
Royal West of England Residential School for the Deaf *EXS* EX2 ..... 2 D6
St Davids CE First School *EXN* EX4 ..... 13 G2
St Georges Hall & Market *EX* EX1 ..... 2 B3
St James High School *EXN* EX4 ..... 9 F4
St James Sports Centre *EXN* EX4 ..... 9 F4
St Johns Caravan & Camping Park *EXM* EX8 ..... 39 F1
St Josephs Catholic Primary School *EXM* EX8 ..... 38 B5
St Loyes School of Occupational Therapy *EXS* EX2 ..... 20 D1
St Lukes High School *EX* EX1 ..... 15 G2
St Margarets School *EX* EX1 ..... 3 H4
St Michaels VA Middle School *EX* EX1 ..... 3 K3
St Nicholas' Priory *EXN* EX4 ..... 2 B4
St Nicholas RC Combined School *EXS* EX2 ..... 2 E6
St Olaves Hotel *EXN* EX4 ..... 2 A3
St Peter's Cathedral *EX* EX1 ..... 2 B3
St Peters CE Aided School *EXS* EX2 ..... 15 G3
St Peters CE Primary School *BUD* EX9 ..... 40 D2
St Peters School *EXM* EX8 ..... 35 E3
St Sidwells CE Combined School *EXN* EX4 ..... 14 A1
St Thomas Cemetery *EXN* EX4 ..... 13 F2
St Thomas First School *EXS* EX2 ..... 13 G4
St Thomas Health Centre *EXS* EX2 ..... 13 F4
St Thomas Shopping Centre *EXN* EX4 ..... 13 G3
St Wilfrids School *EXN* EX4 ..... 13 G2
Southbrook School *EXS* EX2 ..... 21 E1
Southgate Hotel *EX* EX1 ..... 2 C4
Sowton Industrial Estate *EXS* EX2 ..... 16 A3
Starcross Primary School *REXSW* EX6 ..... 36 C4
Starcross Yacht Club *REXSW* EX6 ..... 33 H4
Stoke Hill First School *EXN* EX4 ..... 8 C4
Stoke Hill Middle School *EXN* EX4 ..... 8 C4
Stone Lane Retail Park *EXS* EX2 ..... 13 H5
Summerway Middle School *EXN* EX4 ..... 9 G5
Thorntree Business Units *EXM* EX8 ..... 39 F3
Topsham Museum *TOP/EXT* EX3 ..... 27 F2
Topsham RFC *TOP/EXT* EX3 ..... 22 A5
Topsham Sailing Club *TOP/EXT* EX3 ..... 27 E1
The Topsham School *TOP/EXT* EX3 ..... 27 E1
Topsham Town AFC *TOP/EXT* EX3 ..... 22 A5
Tor College of Nursing *EXS* EX2 ..... 3 H5
Travelodge *EXS* EX2 ..... 16 B4
Tucker's Hall *EXN* EX4 ..... 2 A4
University of Exeter *EXN* EX4 ..... 2 E1
EXN EX4 ..... 7 G3
EXN EX4 ..... 7 G4
University of Exeter (Duryard Halls) *EXN* EX4 ..... 7 G3
University of Exeter (St Luke's Campus) *EX* EX1 ..... 3 F3
University of Exeter (Streatham Campus) *EXN* EX4 ..... 7 H4
EXN EX4 ..... 8 A4
University of Plymouth (Exeter Campus) *EXS* EX2 ..... 20 C1
University of Plymouth (Exmouth Campus) *EXM* EX8 ..... 44 B2
Victoria Park Tennis & Bridge Club *EXS* EX2 ..... 3 G5
Vranch House School *EXN* EX4 ..... 15 F1
Walter Daw First School *EXS* EX2 ..... 15 F4
Warren Golf Club *DAW* EX7 ..... 42 D5
Webbers Farm Caravan & Camping Park *REXNE* EX5 ..... 29 H3
West Exe Technology College *EXS* EX2 ..... 19 G1
Westpoint (Devon County Showground) *REXNE* EX5 ..... 17 E5
Whipton Barton First School *EXN* EX4 ..... 9 F5
Whipton Barton Middle School *EX* EX1 ..... 15 F1
Whipton Hospital *EX* EX1 ..... 15 G1
Willeys Sports Club *EXS* EX2 ..... 2 C7
Willowbrook School *EXN* EX4 ..... 9 F4
Withycombe Raleigh CE Primary School *EXM* EX8 ..... 38 C3
Withycombe RFC *EXM* EX8 ..... 38 B3
Wonford House Hospital *EXS* EX2 ..... 3 K7
Wonford Sports Centre *EXS* EX2 ..... 15 E5
Woodbury CE Primary School *REXNE* EX5 ..... 29 G3
The World of Country Life *EXM* EX8 ..... 45 H1
Wrentham Business Centre *EXN* EX4 ..... 8 B5

Acknowledgements

ost Office is a registered trademark of Post Office Ltd. in the UK and other countries.

ols address data provided by Education Direct.

station information supplied by Johnsons

way street data provided by © Tele Atlas N.V. Tele Atlas

n centre information provided by

n Centre Association Britains best garden centres

ale Garden Centres

tatement on the front cover of this atlas is sourced, selected and quoted
a reader comment and feedback form received in 2004

Notes